GARDEN OPEN TODAY

Open garden day at Sudbrook Cottage; Beverley Nichols looks on
while his factotum, Reginald Gaskin, takes money for charity. Courtesy
of the Bryan Connon Collection.

Daylesford
8·9·05

GARDEN OPEN TODAY

Beverley Nichols

With a Foreword by Roy C. Dicks

TIMBER PRESS
Portland, Oregon

Photographs of Beverley Nichols are the property of
Bryan Connon, reproduced with permission

Drawings by William McLaren

Copyright © 1963 by the estate of Beverley Nichols

First published in 1963 by Jonathan Cape

Foreword and Index copyright © 2002 by Timber Press, Inc.

TIMBER PRESS, INC.
The Haseltine Building
133 S.W. Second Avenue, Suite 450
Portland, Oregon 97204, U.S.A.

ISBN 0-88192-533-0

Printed in Hong Kong

Reprinted 2003

A catalog record for this book is available from the
Library of Congress

CONTENTS

DISCLAIMER

THIS BOOK was originally published in 1963 and mentions many merchants, products, and prices of the time. Few of the nurseries mentioned in the book persist today, and most of the products and trade names are of period interest only. Please note that chemical formulations and applications recommended by Mr. Nichols are of dubious validity today; some are even prohibited by current regulation. Some names of plants have changed in the previous forty years; updated names and synonyms are provided in the index for the reader's convenience. Notwithstanding the above, Mr. Nichols's various enthusiasms and colorful descriptions of plants and gardening practices may be safely regarded as being timeless.

FOREWORD

IN MY INTRODUCTION to the Timber Press reprint of *Laughter on the Stairs* (the second volume of the *Merry Hall* trilogy), I expressed the hope that those books would spark a renewed interest in the garden writings of Beverley Nichols. It appears that they have indeed done so, with Timber regularly going back to press for more copies to fill demand.

There are further indications of the Nichols revival. On the Internet, one can now find hundreds of references to Nichols, from secondhand booksellers to biographical sites and commentaries by devotees. Garden shows, arboretums, and libraries continue to request Nichols readings, and I constantly hear from readers wanting more information about Nichols's other works, his homes, and his life. (Timber Press has aided immensely in this respect by publishing the American edition of Bryan Connon's comprehensive biography, *Beverley Nichols: A Life* (2000), which also includes an updated bibliography of Nichols's works.) Now the republication of *Garden Open Today* should give the revival another boost.

For this book, Nichols wanted to do something different from his previous gardening works. Instead of a semifictional account full of amusing characters, he wanted to write a useful, fact-filled volume based on his thirty years of gardening experience. Although Nichols could not refrain from using humor and anecdote throughout the book, there are certainly many practical observations and suggestions.

There will be few gardeners able to resist the charms of

these whimsical musings and deft descriptions. Keep an eye out for such passages as the ones on how flowers personally tell you where they wish to be planted and the only true method of viewing a snowdrop. If you aren't immediately smitten by such witty observations, perhaps you shouldn't be gardening!

The term "garden open today" originated with the National Gardens Scheme in 1927, when six hundred large private gardens in England were opened on certain days with the entrance fees donated to the Queen's Nursing Institute. Soon the idea caught on with the general public. Anytime one passed a house with a "garden open today" sign on the gate, it was understood that the owners were inviting visitors to view their garden (and to put a small donation in the box hanging nearby).

For Nichols, this book was itself the equivalent of such a sign; on the very last page, he invites the reader to visit Sudbrook Cottage in person. Nichols never withdrew this generous offer to his readers. Many visitors passed through his gate for the next twenty years until his death in 1983. Devotees like myself, who came to know Nichols's works after his death, can only envy those who had such an opportunity, since the cottage has remained a private residence and the gardens have not been kept as Nichols designed them.

Luckily, Eric Grissell, a lifelong Nichols fan, preserved the memories of a 1982 visit to the cottage in his Timber Press book, *Thyme on My Hands* (1986, 169–172). The excerpts below provide a rare eyewitness account and serve as a fitting introduction to Nichols's own descriptions in the ensuing chapters:

> Mr. Nichols took my arm for support and quite cheerfully pointed to his triumphs while I reveled blissfully in

them. . . . We walked slowly past a group of hardy cyclamen blooming in the shadow of the green [garden en-
trance] door; past stately rhododendrons (no die-back
or borer here, in paradise); past tall-flowered sedum
awash with bees and tortoise-shell butterflies on a sea of
pink; past a crimson layer of dahlias held strongly above
their purplish black cloaks (befitting the title 'Bishop of
Llandaff'); beyond the kochia aching to break into
flame at the first sign of fall; beyond the impatiens glowing in the benevolence of the British summer; and ending in the small bed of heathers with their purplish ex-
tremities flung wantonly into the air. It was a simple
selection of flowers, planted as a broad, sweeping curve
backed by an array of entwined conifers. The fore-
ground was an elegant lawn, tightly rolled and closely
clipped putting any putting green to shame.

. . . The two of us had just walked along one of the
sweeping curves which took the edge off the acre-
square, walled garden, and we now had reached the
point where the garden was halved. This was accomplished by the intrusion of a bold curve of conifers into
the lawn. Piercing this green wall were several steps
which were flanked on either side by urns. A path could
be seen above the steps and this appeared to lead directly into a weeping cherry of no little size. . . .

We carefully mounted the steps and followed the path
that now could be seen to veer off to the left of the
cherry tree. The tree itself was rather a surprise as it was
formed from three trees planted tightly together. The
branch structure was so dense as to hide the trunks in
a mound of leaves. Once beyond the cherries we came
upon a small glen and a vista even more ethereal than

the one I'd seen from the doorway. . . . We had come to the edge of a perfectly formal pool set amongst a perfectly informal garden. But what a garden it was . . . a theater in the round, framed against a nearly continuous backdrop of green tapestries. . . . To the left of the pool a planting of white and pale-green foliaged *Cornus* was complemented by a similar *Weigela*; a low-growing spirea added just a blush of pink to the scene. . . . Clumps of Japanese iris rose gracefully through the water's film and these were reflected rather mysteriously by *Crocosmia* planted on the bank. . . . Clusters of starch-white *Anaphalis* jostled the 'Bishop of Llandaff' . . . . And overlooking the entire production was a most handsome specimen of a tall, yellow-foliaged false acacia *Robinia* ×*hillieri*, among the first specimens of its kind to be planted in England. . . .

It was time, now, to begin our trek back towards the green door. We had visited the primary focal points visible from the house . . . . For our return trip the focal point became the house itself, which was framed by an immense canopy of copper beech (one of the few remaining plantings which had come with the house in 1958). Beneath the tree, and subtending a crazy-pavement walk, several irregular clusters of green lay scattered in an informal woodland fashion: a patch of Solomon's Seal gazed diffidently across the way towards the stately *Acanthus*; *Hamamelis* interrupted the lawn in spots; white and green *Lamium* flowed over the ground with an occasional and unsuspected foray upon the boundary of the well-kept lawn. . . . It was but a short walk along the path, or so it seemed, and too soon we had reached the drawing room door. Mr. Nichols

begged his leave to rest a moment and ready himself for
yet another set of visitors.

With these images in mind, turn the page and allow Mr.
Nichols to conduct you on your own personal tour.

ROY C. DICKS
Raleigh, North Carolina

GARDEN OPEN TODAY

Facsimile of the Original Edition of 1963

Homo
sapiens
flori
bundus

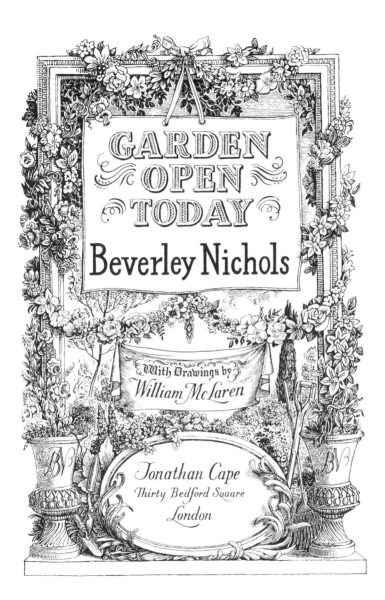

GARDEN
OPEN
TODAY

Beverley Nichols

With Drawings by
William McLaren

Jonathan Cape
Thirty Bedford Square
London

CONTENTS

For
Kenneth Page
To whom the Garden and its owner
owe a lasting debt

BY WAY OF INTRODUCTION

WITH a very few exceptions, all the flowers extolled in the following pages may be inspected—or perhaps I should say 'verified'—in my own garden on Ham Common in the County of Surrey.

I mention this because critics have sometimes accused me of wandering down garden paths which never really existed, under pergolas of prose which were wreathed only in the blossoms of my fancy.

This is not the case. There may have been moments when one gilded the lily, but by and large the flowers of which I have written have been flowers that I have grown myself. And though there may also have been moments when 'whimsy' has entered into my description of them, I do not share the fashionable conviction that 'whimsy' is the ultimate literary sin, provided that it springs naturally from the temperament of the author. It might not be a bad idea if some of the critics who use 'whimsy' as an excuse for berating so many authors who have delighted the world, from Lamb to Barrie, were to remind themselves what the word really means. According to the Oxford Dictionary one who is 'whimsical' is, 'fantastic, fanciful, characterized by deviation from the ordinary'. These qualities are not specially deplorable, and even if they were, it would make not the smallest difference to me, nor to my way of looking at things.

However, this is not a whimsical compilation; though the fingers that wrote it may have been 'precious', they were also, more often than not, extremely dirty. Gardening gloves may be all very well in their way, but in so many tasks, like weeding, one has literally to take the gloves off. Only one's own nails and fingers can deal, for example, with the sinister little bulbous roots of *Oxalis floribunda*, and only naked arms plunged in up to the elbows can tackle the slimy, sucking growths that have attached themselves to the sides of the lily pond by the time that autumn comes. It is not a pleasant job, it is probably bad for one's Chopin, and there is always the hideous possibility that one's fingers may inadvertently fasten round a newt; but it is the sort of job that the owner of the garden has to do himself, for the simple reason that nobody else will do it.

I hope that the amateur may find here some useful suggestions, if only because his attention will be called to a number of flowers with which he is unfamiliar. I have been gardening now for over thirty years, I have prowled round parks and pleasances in many corners of the earth and have read as widely as most; and yet, still they come, the new discoveries, the unknown beauties, like fresh young dancers who suddenly drift on to the stage as the ballet is drawing to its close. An example of these discoveries is described in Chapter Twelve, 'And The Whites'. How was it possible that for thirty years I had never seen, nor even heard of the galtonia, which might be described as a giant lily of the valley four feet high, wax-white, giving an icy gleam to the border in the sultry heart of summer? And why, even more strangely, did so many of the great bulb merchants—the firms which cater for at least ninety per cent of the gardening public—omit it from their catalogues? What was the reason for this curious conspiracy? If the galtonia were exotic or 'difficult' one could understand the neglect, but it is hardy and of the greatest amiability, flourishing in sunshine or semi-shade, on most types of soil. Nor are the bulbs expensive, if you know where to get them.

'If you know where to get them.' Which reminds me. I have thought it wise to include an appendix listing the names of nurseries where you may obtain plants or seeds of the rarer flowers which are recommended. Doubtless, this will be misinterpreted, and I shall be accused of getting a 'rake-off'. Alas, this is not so. I long to get a 'rake-off', but I do not know how one goes about these things. True, there was an occasion, after an article on gardening tools, when a very large German firm sent me a rake without the 'off'. It was a patent one, and it was all for free. This gave me an agreeable feeling of corruption. But when we tried it out on the paths it immediately got clogged up with leaves and emitted a hissing noise which frightened the cats, so I refrained from mentioning it in my 'column'. Again, after an article on weeding, a gigantic organization kindly presented me with a small bag of faintly rancid dandelion-killer, which made holes in the lawn, but had no effect on the dandelions. That is about the sum total of my 'rake-offs'. The only time I received a really princely present was when the King of the Lily World, whose name is Jan de Graaf, sent me from Oregon a glittering Cinderella box of American lilies. These, admittedly, I have written about, not in the hope of more favours to come, but simply because I could not help myself. They are the sort of flowers that one wants not only to write about but to set to music.

Is there anything else before we begin? Yes—a word about 'experts'. In this book I come into fairly frequent conflict with these 'experts', from the Royal Horticultural Society downwards. I am all for abiding by the rules, and it is foolish not to read the directions on the packet, but if ever there was a place where rules were made to be broken, it is in the garden.

However, there is more to it than that, and it is all summed up in the old expression 'green fingers'. This I believe to be not just a poetical fancy but a physical fact. In the chapter entitled 'Mysteries', I have suggested that just as there are fingers which, for certain forms of plant life, are 'green', so there may be fingers which, for other forms, are 'black'. As yet, we have scarcely begun to explore the subtle relationship between plants and men. All we know is that it consists in a form of 'vibrations'. These vibrations can be so powerful that in some recent experiments in Paris a cut rose was made to wilt by the prolonged playing of a saxophone—an experience I have shared myself. However, we do not know whence these vibrations emanate nor to what extent they are influenced by the human agency behind them. If instead of the saxophonist the rose had been treated to Menuhin playing Elgar's Violin Concerto the results might have been very different.

Does this mean that gardening is a question of hit or miss, and that all one has to do is to think beautiful thoughts and open the window of the music-room so that the sweet strains of the 'Moonlight Sonata' may drift out and shame the blight off the roses? Certainly not. Whatever the colour of your fingers, you will never grow a rhododendron on an alkaline soil. You must at least *begin* by following 'the directions on the packet', and in this little packet of a book there are plenty of directions, which are the result of hard-won experience. But in the long run, when you have abided by some rules and—quite rightly—broken others, you will have learned the greatest lesson of all, which is summed up in a pretty phrase that has drifted down the long labyrinths of anonymous English prose, 'Love makes things grow the greenest'.

GARDEN OPEN TODAY

CHAPTER ONE

FRAMEWORK

THE greater part of this book will be concerned with those of my own favourite flowers that are not too widely known by the general public. It will also, when necessary, tell how to grow them and where to get them.

However, descriptions of flowers suspended, as it were, in space are apt to be boring, at any rate to me. I want to know where they are growing, in what sort of soil, in what aspect, and who looks after them, for how many days of the week. This is the very least of the information which one needs to make flowers come to life, and one very seldom gets it. If the writer also cares to throw in a few details as to whether the gardener has rheumatism and whether the walls are occasionally festooned with neighbouring pussies, so much the better.

In short, I want a frame for the picture, and in this chapter we will try to hammer one out.

My garden abuts on to Ham Common, which is neither the heart of the country nor the edge of the suburbs, but a happy compromise between the two. If you turn to the left outside the front door, you have only to walk fifty yards to reach the silver birch woods that extend to the gates of Richmond Park. These woods abound in birds, for the park has many sanctuaries, and sometimes I feel that we are almost overbirded, particularly when the screech owls are up to their tricks at night outside the bedroom window, giving a life-like impersonation of the mad scene from Lucia, as sung by Madame Never-Mind-Who. We are also frequently visited by pairs of wild duck, who descend like dive-bombers on to the pond, to the detriment of the lilies.

The garden itself is just under an acre. It stretches round a long, rambling cottage built in 1800, and is surrounded on three sides by high walls of mellow brick. On the fourth side is a fence giving on to the neighbouring garden, which we may ignore, because we are shut off from it by groups of trees. In the distance, through a tracery of giant beech and oak, we can dimly discern the fairy tale outlines of an old Queen Anne house, built with bricks made in the little factory of Daniel Defoe before he wrote *Robinson Crusoe*.

A pleasant 'ambience', you will agree.

Now for the soil. This is a vital point in any garden and for me, in this garden, especially so. For the soil is acid—meaning, of course, that it contains no chalk—and this is the first time that I have had a garden which was not pocked with that loathsome substance. At long last I can grow rhododendrons, azaleas, heathers, eucryphias, blue hydrangeas and all the other darlings to whom chalk is death. Apart from its mercifully acid character, the soil is fair to middling, light and sandy, so that we have to do a great deal of watering.

Finally, the labour. I am fortunate in having the services of Mr Page, whom you will be meeting. Of all the gardeners I have ever had, he is by far the most knowledgeable, with a scholarly understanding of every form of British plant life, and a keen, inquiring mind. He comes on Tuesdays and Wednesdays and also on Saturday mornings, arriving on a motor-bicycle looking rather fierce in a white helmet.

Gaskin, my factotum, does the lawns, and I do the fiddly bits which nobody else has time for—dead-heading the rhododendrons, weeding the heather beds, disentangling the *Clematis tangutica* and retying it to the firethorn, etc. etc.

That is the total labour force, apart from the cats, who are tireless in their rearrangement of seedling beds and their daily stripping of the bark off the fruit trees.

*   *   *

It is time that we described the design of the garden, which is not only severely practical but quite exceptionally pretty. Perhaps I should not say this, as I was responsible for it—not forgetting many admirable suggestions from Mr Page. However, everybody else says it, and apparently means it, so we will let it pass. It is one of those gardens which has developed like a piece of music, in a series of melodic lines.

But when I took possession, in the summer of 1958, there was nothing in the least melodic about it. On the contrary we had to start from scratch. I was faced by a gaunt rectangle

23

so planned that its gauntness was accentuated, and so planted that almost everything in the beds had to be torn up and thrown on to the rubbish heap. Round the walls there were straight rows of shocking pink phlox fighting it out with triangles of diseased golden rod. Across the lawn there was a sharp ugly line of aubretia clambering over dreadful little speckly rocks. Most of the fruit trees were dying, most of the roses were dead, and to crown the melancholy spectacle was a giant topiary bird bang in the middle of the lawn; it was the size of a motor-car, hacked out of box. The removal of this bird was like exorcising an evil spirit. We gave it to an eccentric friend, who took it away in a lorry. The bird fell out, striking terror into the hearts of passing motorists, and causing a traffic block for miles around.

Our first few months, therefore, were spent in scraping the canvas clean, creating a blank space on which to impose a pattern. Not for the first time in my life! And this makes me think that here might be a fitting place to say a few words on the general principle of garden design.

I have been designing gardens for over thirty years. Perhaps the best measure of their success—here you must be prepared for a quite shameless piece of trumpet blowing—is that those who have come after me have left them precisely as they found them, for the very simple reason that they could not think of any way of improving them. This does not imply that one is a God-given genius who has only to walk into a garden and wave a magic wand in order to create beauty out of chaos. Nothing so tiresome. It merely implies that one has perhaps given more thought to the problems of design than most of one's contemporaries, even the professionals. By 'thought' I mean hard unremitting thought, day after day, night after night, tramping up and down the lawn, standing in corners and staring till the shadows fall, making little dummy paths with bamboo sticks, taking them up again, and again, and again, drawing, painting, even building temporary walls of loose brick—all in the search of a perfection that will not only delight the eye but take into account the hard facts of soil and shelter and climate. For the analogy of the 'clean canvas' was perhaps a false one; no gardener has so simple a substance on which to draw. The design he imposes must be constantly modified and sometimes totally transformed by a hand stronger than his own—the hand of Nature. Maybe the art of gardening is simply the knowledge of how to hold that hand, and how to clasp it in friendship.

*　　*　　*

Three main principles of garden design have emerged from all these years of thought. They are quite arbitrary but that should be the nature of principles, if they are to serve any useful purpose.

1. A garden without water is not a garden at all. Even a back-yard should have a miniature water-lily in a tub.
2. You double the size of a garden by cutting it in half.
3. The beauty of a square garden begins with the creation of curves, and the beauty of a circular or irregular garden begins with the creation of squares or rectangles. It is a question of the harmonious blending of the two. This, of course, is the pervading principle of the architecture of Sir Christopher Wren, who, in his turn, developed it from Palladio.

Let us begin by discussing this water business.

1. To me, water in a garden has far more than a decorative importance. It is not merely a splash of silver against a green background; it has a mystic quality. Even the smallest pool gives to the garden a fourth dimension. It is like a mirror in a room, opening the wall to ghostly chambers that you will never enter. A pool does more than that. It beckons a patch of the heavens down to the earth. One is heavy and oppressed, walking across the lawn one's feet drag slowly, one reaches the pool, and stares into the water. And then, even in winter when the lilies are sleeping, something seems to happen. The clouds float at one's feet across the steely surface, the bare branches of the copper beech have the delicate perfection of a Chinese drawing, a bird skims the water, tracing a single exquisite curve, and round the little statue in the centre is spread a liquid tapestry of purest blue. Here is a province of its own, a place of retreat and solitude, where the world's alarms are far away.

Throughout this book—like signposts warning me that certain pens are apt to run away with themselves—you will find, in capital letters, the words PRACTICAL NOTES. This might therefore be the occasion to observe that water introduces the gardener to a whole new world of floral delights, some of which you will find described in a later part of the book.

So much for the first principle. The manner in which we applied it to the present garden is discussed in the next chapter.

2. Doubling the size of the garden by cutting it in half.

Although this may sound like a paradox, it is plain common sense. A garden is a picture; every picture has a focal point, and if, as it wanders towards the focal point, the eye can be diverted, the picture is thereby apparently enlarged. I hate to ask you, but perhaps you might care to read that last sentence again? The key to it lies in the word 'diverted'. The human eye is easily led astray; indeed, this is the beginning in life, of most of our follies, and in the garden, of most of our delights. Every garden path can be magically extended if it is made to take a sudden turn to the right or to the left. Which means that somewhere in its course it must encounter a wall, a cluster of trees, even a wooden fence, set there to provoke the aforesaid eye, to intrigue it, to make one ask the ultimate question—what lies beyond?

For every garden, surely, should be to some extent a secret garden? Even in stately homes of many acres the magic lies not so much in a grand parade of terraces or a noble sweep of lawns as in the faint gleam of silver from a distant lake, half hidden by the trees. It is to such a prospect that the eye dances in delight, demanding more.

Cutting my present garden in half presented a number of problems which will be also described in the next chapter. In the meantime . . .

PRACTICAL NOTE

The foregoing paragraphs may suggest that this second principle is merely an airy idea for the diversion of the rich; it is—or should be—the concern of all those who have suburban oblongs. On my journeys to London by the district railway I pass hundreds of these oblongs, and only rarely pass any of them designed with imagination. If their owners would only cut the wretched things in half, *then* something might begin—then there might be written the opening lines of a poem.

To make this plain, here is a diagram to illustrate one of

the simplest of the many ways in which this division may be accomplished at a very modest cost.

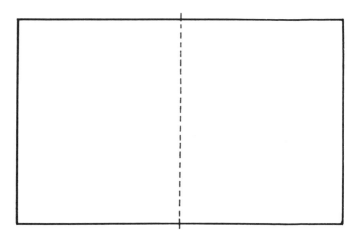

3. Our third principle, concerning the relation of curves and squares, may sound obscure, but is, in fact, very obvious. Every time that a gardener takes a spade and breaks the monotony of a straight border by coming boldly out into the lawn, and then turns in a long graceful sweep till he almost comes back to the wall or the fence, he is employing this principle.

However, even as I wrote those words I wondered . . . how often *does* the average gardener make these sweeps and curves? Very seldom. The men who write about gardens never tire of telling us to follow Nature and to copy Nature's secrets; indeed, you would think that Nature was a personal friend, with a private telephone number, to whom only they had access. But when I visit their gardens I have a feeling that Nature cannot have had very much to say to them.

Whoever saw a straight border designed by Nature? When did Nature learn the habits of the drill sergeant? Except in gardens of deliberately planned formality, straight borders are not only offensive to the eye, but impractical and uneconomic. Look at it like this. Suppose that you plant at the back of the border a group of philadelphus. As it grows, the philadelphus throws out its arms in a series of gestures that may be exquisite but gradually swamp the flowers in front. What do you do? Cut off the arms of the poor creature? Certainly not; you move the flowers in front further out on to the lawn. And if, when you do so, you allow the philadelphus to instruct you where to put them, you will not go far wrong. The great majority of the flowers in my garden are in their present places because they have personally informed me, in the clearest possible tones, that this is where they wish to be. Listening to flowers is one of the most important of all the gardener's duties.

This section will have no supplement of PRACTICAL NOTES because the whole of it, as I hope you will agree, is strictly practical.

And now for the application of these principles in Chapter Two.

THE PICTURE

I SAID in the last chapter that a pond is a mystic thing, but this does not mean that it is a mysterious thing; the two adjectives belong to different worlds whatever the dictionary may say about it. A hen's egg is mystic but it is not mysterious; although men have argued for centuries about which came first you can still go out and buy it at the grocer's. So it is with ponds; they hold a depth of unwritten music, they mirror great masterpieces of sky and cloud, but they are created very simply, with spades, the sweat of the brow, and water from the tap.

So it was with ours. Beginning with our first principle that water is essential, and linking it to our third principle that squares must be complemented by circles, I eventually decided, after many hours of concentration, that a large round hole must be dug in the centre of the further lawn. The decision may have had mystic origins but there was nothing at all mysterious about the procedure. We merely got hold of some friends and dug a hole.

Odd as it may seem, this is the best way of making a pond, unless you live in a stately home and have a sudden urge to flood the park. Simply dig a hole two feet deep and get the man round the corner to line it with cement. My own is perhaps rather more elaborate than that, for round the circumference is a thin circle of old brick, flush with the grass. (This circle is edged with a continuous line of pale blue crocuses so that in the spring the pond is formally framed in flowers.) In the centre is a lead cherub holding a vase which spouts a tiny jet on to the surface with a pleasant tinkle of sharps and trebles. However, these are 'extras'; you can have great delight without them.

People seeing the pond for the first time say: 'But wasn't it a terrible business putting the pipes under the lawn?'

To which the answer is: 'There are no pipes.'

'Then how is it filled?'

'By water from the hose. When it evaporates in hot weather we top it up again.'

'Doesn't it overflow in a rainy season?'

'No. It runs off into a soakaway, and nothing could be simpler than a soakaway.'

Finally: 'Doesn't it get very dirty?'

'Yes. It gets absolutely filthy.'

'So what do you do about *that*?'

'I ring up the fire-brigade.'

This answer usually surprises them. Indeed, I was also surprised on first learning that one of the functions of the gallant British fire-brigades is to clean out ornamental ponds for amateur gardeners. It sounded almost too good to be true—as though one could telephone to the Foreign Office and engage an under-secretary to wait at table. (At some dinner-parties, nowadays, one suspects that this is what one's hostess has actually done.) Anyway, one can and one does ring up the fire-brigade, and they come along in their own good time. I doubt if they would come if they were coping with the local Woolworth's actually blazing on the other side of the road; one cannot expect civil servants to have any real sense of the priorities. But if nothing is on fire they come, and they drag an enormous hose across the lawn and put it into the pond. Out gurgles the dirty water, and after about an hour one is slipping about the slimy floor catching the fish, who greatly resent the whole business, though they seem to come to no harm through it.

When the firemen have gone (the money they get goes to one of their charities) all one has to do is to scrape away the accumulated weeds of the year, leaving just enough for the fish to nibble. There will be buckets and buckets of weeds, which should be thrown straight on to the compost heap, for they are exceptionally rich in organic matter. Finally, refill, and you will have a crystal clear pond for the following year.

All this may sound faintly bizarre to some people—particularly to those who believe what they read in the advertisements. These are constantly announcing magic potions which clear the pond with a single bottle. I have tried most of them, with absolutely no effect. And whatever the fish-men may tell you about fish keeping a pond clean, disbelieve it; fish do *not* keep ponds clean. Period. Even if they did, why deny yourself the pleasure of meeting a charming band of gallant gentlemen whom you would probably never otherwise encounter? Unless, of course, they happened to be dragging you down a ladder by the scruff of the neck.

*   *   *

The pond, then, was the starting point of the whole design—the circle within the square. Of the lilies that it was to harbour, and the water plants that were to cluster round its edge, I write later. Meanwhile, let us see where we went from here.

One of the laws of Nature is that if you dig a hole you thereby create a mountain. This was precisely what I wanted—a sufficient volume of earth to create the illusion of a slope. A level garden can be very beautiful, but this was not the sort of garden I had planned.

But where was the slope to be? One was faced with a blank canvas, apart from the aforesaid circle, and a huge irregular mound of earth.

I decided that this was the moment to forget about our first principle—water—and to concentrate on the second—cutting the garden in half. Sooner or later it would have to be cut in half. Sooner or later the line would have to be drawn—the line of mystery and expectation. Why not now?

Which brings us to the urns. Not for the first time, the urns would have to be brought out of the tool-shed, and placed in the strategic centre of the stage, wherever that centre might eventually proclaim itself.

This demands a word of explanation.

I have two very beautiful porphyry urns which have played a leading role in all my gardens, and they have always been the cause of trouble. They weigh a ton; it takes ages to decide where to put them; and none of my tougher friends will give them even so much as a passing glance. They smile coldly, and sooner or later the word 'rupture' rears its ugly head.

What is one to do? It is vital that the urns should be properly placed, with the most delicate exactitude. This means that one must sit in chairs, for hours on end, while urn-carriers pass before one, as on a Greek frieze. But where are the urn-carriers of today? How does one find them? Certainly not by advertising. 'Strong young men needed to walk round a gentleman's lawn, carrying urns . . .' Such a *cri de cœur*, in these days, might be gravely misinterpreted.

However, eventually I found the urn-carriers, and both of them were jet black, and both of them caught cold, because naturally, there were occasions when they had to stand stock still for quite a long time in a piercing wind, groaning under these great weights. But in the end we decided upon the right place, which was—ironically enough– in the dead centre of the lawn, to within an inch. Which only goes to show that one's eye is not such a bad judge. And the urn-carriers departed from my life like two strange black shadows, sneezing, largely reimbursed, and inflamed by generous potions of their own Jamaican rum.

I wonder what has happened to them today? I should not be surprised to learn that they were running a profitable landscape-gardening business in Notting Hill Gate.

*   *   *

The picture is taking shape.

We have a bold silver circle of water at the far end of the lawn. We have our very beautiful urns in the centre, standing on pediments of old brick, about three feet high.

The rest is a blank. A bleak, square blank. All one knows is that there must be curves and circles and colour.

But how are these to be achieved?

This is where I hope to prove the truth of my assertion that a practical gardener must 'listen' to what his flowers and his trees are saying. For the lower half of the garden was dominated by a gigantic copper beech which converses night and day, in the most charming accents. On gusty mornings, when the wind swept across the common, it was positively voluble, and even on quiet autumn evenings, when the nuts fell on to the lawn with an explosive patter from the branches of the walnut tree with which its own arms were linked, there were delicate sighs and hints and whispers. As yet I could not interpret them, though I spent hours prowling round in its shadow, 'listening'.

It was not till a brilliant morning in the following March that the copper beech—having presumably come to the conclusion that this impasse had lasted long enough—suddenly decided to speak clearly. I drew up the window and looked out on to the silver lawn. The picture was very beautiful, like a heraldic shield—argent for the lawn, sable for the shadow under the tree. I made a mental note to remember something that gardeners are often inclined to forget—the fickle, flimsy character of Jack Frost and the absurdly simple techniques that can outwit him. Under the beech there was no frost at all; no silver sheen, merely a dark circle of unchilled earth. The light airy superstructure of branch and twig had been enough to guard it against all the sharp, stinging arrows of the night.

I stayed there by the window, thinking that I really must get a piece of paper and write this down—the way in which you can beat this frost business by the most delicate methods.

Even a piece of fish-net, strung above a bed of tender plants, is enough protection. Jack Frost is a foolish enemy, treacherous but stupid, and apt to expend his venom on the flimsiest defence. Even a spider's web is enough.

I pushed on a thick dressing-gown and some gum shoes, went downstairs, and stepped out on to the lawn. The shoes made dark tracks on the crisp grass, and I thought that this would be a wonderful way to sketch out a design, using one's feet like charcoal, if only there were some sort of plan in one's head. I walked all round the shadow, and as I came full circle, the copper beech suddenly spoke. It said . . .

But no, that would be really going too far; if we allow the copper beech to talk we shall have gnomes climbing up the hollyhocks before we can say knife. So let us merely note that this was the moment when—because of the freaks of the frost and the natural protection of the tree—the whole design of the garden fell dramatically into shape.

Here was a bold dark circle which must be made permanent, and the obvious way to make it permanent was by planting it with evergreens.

But here was something more—a place of shadow and shelter where I should be able to grow many of the more delicate rhododendrons, which in any other part of the garden would be scorched by the sun at noon or shrivelled by the frost at night.

Finally, here was a snag, which has probably already suggested itself to the intelligent reader. Rhododendrons will not grow under beeches. Indeed, almost nothing will grow under them except certain bulbs, and a few shade-loving ground plants such as periwinkle and St John's Wort. The vast majority of shrubs pine away, throttled by the surrounding roots. And it is useless to try to save them with peat; the beech gobbles it all up as soon as you lay it down.

The manner in which we surmounted this problem was so simple and yet (sound of trumpets, off !) so ingenious, that it deserves a section to itself.

*   *   *

All we did was to dig a two-foot trench in a wide circle round the tree, thereby 'impounding' the roots, which are very shallow. Having done this, we got a load of concrete blocks, which we stood up on end in the trench, forming a little wall against which the beech's roots would struggle in vain. After which there was nothing to do but clean the earth on our side of the trench, replenish with peat, and plant our rhododendrons.

When I first mooted this plan to my gardening friends they all, without exception, prophesied disaster.

'You realize, of course, that you will kill the copper beech?' said some.

To which the answer is that after five years the copper beech is healthier, sturdier and glossier than it ever was before.

'You realize that the roots will get *under* the concrete, and that after a year you will be exactly where you started?' said others. They had something there; fortunately it was a very small something. After three years a few fibrous roots did begin to creep under the concrete. But it only needed an hour's work with a sharp spade to chop them off.

There was another school of thought whose members sighed and asked, in pained tones, if I did not think that the whole thing was rather 'unnatural'?

The word 'unnatural' always enrages me. What does it

mean? *I* am 'unnatural'; I have two false teeth and I did not find either of them growing on the lawn. *You* are 'unnatural' every time you visit the barber. And if ever there was an 'unnatural' thing, God wot, it is a garden. The only 'natural' gardens are those which are covered with weeds and choked with brambles. Learn from Nature, by all means, commune with Nature, take Nature for long and earnest walks down the garden path, but do for heaven's sake keep the blessed creature under control.

This was all I was doing in the case of the copper beech. Keeping it under control. The result has been triumphantly successful, as you can see for yourself, if you care to come and look.

PRACTICAL NOTE

(This title, not for the first time, is inserted for the benefit of those readers who feel that they have no time for the ecstasies and only want hard facts.)

Here goes.

If I am ever remembered with any small degree of gratitude by the owners of gardens—particularly of small gardens —it will be because I was probably the first person to draw their attention to the possibilities of intelligent root-pruning. In tens of thousands of gardens there are little deserts which might be made to blossom like the rose. These deserts are the blank patches under old trees—trees which nobody has the heart to cut down. Sometimes, so pervasive are their roots that the bare patches stretch far out on to the lawn. True, as I indicated above, there are a few things that can compete with these roots, such as periwinkles, but one does not want to spend one's entire life wreathed in periwinkles, even if one turns them into wine which—*en passant*—is a potent emetic.

Generally speaking, it is safe to prune the roots of smaller trees to a radius of six feet from the trunk. After I had finished the copper beech experiment a kind friend allowed me to repeat it in his own garden with a laburnum and a mountain ash, each about twenty years old. They were drastically pruned to a radius of four feet. They are both flourishing, after five years, and so are the flowers he has planted in their shadow.

* * *

By devious methods, we seem at last to have drawn our design, to have squared our circles, and circled our squares.

Maybe all that I have been trying to say was said much better, two thousand years ago, by an unknown Chinese poet who wrote:

> In all arts and industry, all human affairs and relations, the combination of the straight and the curved makes for the best results. In archery, the bow is bent, but the arrow is straight. In a boat, the mast must be straight, while the hook is curved, and in carpentry and masonry, you have to have both the straight guiding line and the T square, and the compass. Sometimes it is better to give a sly hint than straight advice to a friend, and Kings and rulers can be made to see your point by a covered, indirect analogy better than by straightforward counsel.[1]

How pleasant it would be for any author to hold in his fingers a pen as delicate and subtle as that of the wise man who wrote those words! As things are, we must continue to

[1] *The Importance of Understanding*, by Lin Yutang, William Heinemann, Ltd.

do our best with the blunt instrument in the hand of the present author.

Which suggests that this might be a good place to draw a plan, to put all these words into the form of a picture, if we can find somebody to interpret them. We shall be wandering round the garden for quite a while together, poking our noses into all sorts of odd corners, and we shall want to know whether those corners are in sun or shade, which way the wind blows, whether there are roots to be reckoned with, or the drip of eaves, or even the occasional intrusion of pussies, native or foreign.

Perhaps it might even be a good idea to have several plans, beginning with one like this, as seen from a helicopter.

This aerial view reveals two small front gardens, which we have not previously mentioned. Let us say a word about these, beginning with the little square patch outside the porch.

When I took possession this patch was dominated by another of those gigantic topiary birds, even larger, blacker, more sinister and more diseased than the one on the main lawn at the back.

I observed to friends that it was like living in a sort of nightmare aviary.

'But you can't take it down,' they said.

'Why not?'

'The cottage is Crown property and you're not allowed to do any structural alterations.'

'What is there structural about this beastly bird?'

'Well, maybe not structural. But you're not allowed to cut down trees. Particularly trees like this.'

'What do you mean by "trees like this"?'

'It's part of the landscape. It must have been here at least

three hundred years. It's probably historic. For all you know Queen Anne may have sat under it.'

I suggested that whatever Queen Anne may have done under it would hardly account for its expression of permanent malevolence. All the same, I was slightly disturbed.

However, the bird had to go, and it went—on a wild wet evening in October; and as we hacked through the last of the tough, wiry trunk I swear that there was an extra flurry in the wind and a hiss of angry wings in the darkening sky. Certainly, a moment later there was a great clutter and commotion in the rookery over the way, as though a dark, spectral visitor had suddenly flown in to disturb the peace.

Nobody said anything; no fusspots complained; and at last we were able to plan this little plot. Here there were no problems of design; it was merely a question of finding the right lead figure for the centure, making the utmost use of the three sheltered beds, and paving the rest of it.

The same general plan was adopted for the two strips running round the rest of the house. If more labour had been available I might not have had so much paving; it would have been pleasant to contrive a tiny cottage garden—a tangle of madonna lilies, bergamot, Mrs Sinkins pinks, and other simple delights. But it would have been impossible to keep tidy. Besides, one can have a great deal of fun with paving plants for an absolute minimum of labour if one uses them intelligently, as we shall see in the course of the narrative.

So much for the front garden.

The main garden, I hope, speaks for itself. But here again, a new feature is revealed—the 'annex' in the top right-hand corner. This is kindly rented to me by the grace and favour of my next-door neighbour, Mrs Poyser, who is everybody's ideal next-door neighbour in the sense that our communications are almost entirely of a floral nature, and that our respective cats, though not exactly buddies, are at least prepared to respect each other's rights. Indeed, one of hers, by name Webster, has recently been observed on several occasions in deep conversation under the walnut tree with one of mine, by name 'Five'. If anything important develops from these conversations as we tell our story, the reader will naturally be informed.

This little annex is invaluable for the compost heap, the bonfire, the frames, the herb garden, and the cutting beds, none of which could conveniently have been fitted into the design of the main garden. I do not think that Mrs Poyser really wanted me to have it, but she was given clearly to understand that she might have had a suicide on her hands if she didn't, so she did.

And now, at last, we can begin to talk about the flowers themselves.

Snowdrop single and double

Primula denticulata

Pulmonaria augustifolia

CHAPTER THREE

FIRSTLINGS

IT will be generally agreed that the only way in which we can appreciate the beauty of snowdrops is by going out into the garden, lying flat on our backs in the mud, and gazing up at them from below.

Only thus can we savour the delicacy of a design in which pale green ribbons are painted round bells of icy white. Snowdrops are flowers that you have to hold up, and look into, if you want to get to know them.

Which brings us to the Nichols' Snowdrop Invention.

This is what you do.

You cut out a sheet of mirror so that it fits into a bowl, or a basket, or a box. In this sheet of mirror, you cut three or four circular holes which should be just a little smaller than the smallest of your pinholders. (Or rather, the little man round the corner does these things. If he does them as cheaply and as quickly as he did them for me, you will have nothing to complain about.)

After which, all you have to do is to fill the bowl with water, arrange the pinholders so that they correspond with the holes above them, replace the mirror, and stick in the snowdrops.

Thereupon, you will find that you have created a floral fairy story. The snowdrops seem to be growing in a silver lake—white echoes white, green echoes green, as they gaze for the first time at their own beauty. And though it may be nadir of whimsy to suggest that on their faces there is an air of delighted surprise, that is my theory and I am sticking to it.

You must exercise your own ingenuity in choosing the container for this device. You will have a wide choice, because mirrors are very easy to cut. One day I want to get my man round the corner to contrive a mirrored top for a small round table, which could be used for a diversity of flowers, and moved from room to room.

There is only one drawback to the Nichols' Snowdrop Invention. If you use it in very warm rooms the snowdrops will droop. But in a moderate temperature they will last almost as long as out of doors.

*   *   *

Like so many other flowers the modern snowdrop is 'going places', having stood still for many centuries. During those centuries their lovers have serenaded them in the most melodious manner; no other flower has so many charming local names, particularly in the West Country. Down in Somerset the villagers still call them Eve's Tears, in Devonshire they are Dewdrops, in Wiltshire they are Dinglebells and in some parts of Cornwall Naked Maidens. In many parts of England, if you are lucky, you can hear the phrase—casually dropped in bucolic conversation—the Shakespearean February Fair Maids, though it is usually abbreviated to Fairmaids.

However, as I observed, the modern snowdrop is 'going places'; the lists of new introductions in the bulb catalogues grow longer and longer—and the prices, too. So maybe the last lingering echoes of these antique endearments will soon have died away for ever. We must regret their passing, though we welcome the lovely newcomers. In a modest way I have experimented with some of these. But before mentioning them let us say a few words in general about the planting of snowdrops.

*　　*　　*

In order that these words may have complete authority I will quote from a letter recently received during a long and appropriately impassioned correspondence with the biggest and best grower of the biggest and best snowdrops in the world.

It cannot be too *strongly* advocated, writes this learned person, that the *vast* majority of snowdrops should be planted in the *Spring*, in the *green*. We feel this so *deeply* that apart from special orders we do not lift stock for autumn sale *at all*. Snowdrops should not remain out of the ground a *moment* longer than is necessary. *Double* snowdrops in particular are retarded to a *drastic* extent; indeed, if *Galanthus nivalis flore pleno* is allowed to become *really dry*, which is *criminal*, they will only flower 25%, whereas if moved *green*, they will flower 75% in the next spring. We *earnestly* hope that you will use your influence to drive this point *home* to your *many* readers.

This is the sort of business letter that I find very suitable. And it *is* a 'business' letter, because the man who wrote it has —quite rightly—climbed to fortune up the green stems of many million flowers, simply because he knows his job. The italics, I *hasten* to say, are *not* my own. But they give the letter a delightfully Victorian flavour; one can almost hear the rustle of the royal pen dashing off a note to Disraeli, to thank him for the primroses that smile at her on the royal desk. If italics are employed at all, they should be laid on thickly, like icing on a wedding cake. And maybe it would be well for the world if they were employed more often. The strain and stress of events surely demands an equal strain and stress in the communications of diplomacy.

However, the somewhat breathless tone of this communication must not distract our attention from the sound sense of the argument it points. Snowdrops *are*—this is getting infectious!—best planted 'in the green'. The ideal way to come by them, of course, is to dig up deep clumps in the woods, with so much soil that there is no root disturbance whatsoever. As this is rarely possible for most people, the next best thing is to order them from a reliable firm for delivery in early spring. They will arrive looking very dilapidated, with all the green leaves bruised and drooping, but when they flower the following year they will give a far braver display than if you had invested in a nice little collection of nut-brown bulbs with a pretty picture on the packet.

PRACTICAL NOTE

The finest, earliest, and safest snowdrop at a reasonable

price is *Galanthus elwesii*, and this is a variety that *can* be planted from dried bulbs, in the autumn. You might as well realize the reason for this. It is simply because, unlike our native snowdrops, the bulbs have been so well baked and ripened—mostly in Turkey—that they have stored up enough sunshine to enable them to withstand the uprooting to colder climes.

But even this obliging and exquisite flower is not foolproof if it is wrongly treated. The vital thing to remember is that it should be planted in full sunshine. So many people, associating snowdrops with the white drifts that they have seen in our own woodlands, assume that all snowdrops are creatures of the shade. But *elwesii* is definitely a creature of the sun and if you put it in the shade it will die.

The snowdrop family is larger and more varied than many people realize. In my own garden you will find three varieties so beautiful that they take much of the sting out of winter. They are:

The scented snowdrop: this grows a foot high and disposes on the airs of January a faint tinge of magnolia blossom.

The autumn snowdrop: this flowers in early November and pushes its spikes through the earth before the leaves appear.

The green double snowdrop: the name explains itself.

Admittedly, none of these three varieties is in large supply, for they are expensive. I have planted them in a special corner—the sort of corner which, in the manner of Barrie's magic island, 'likes to be visited'.

The brutal commercial details, together with the rather intimidating Latin names, will be found in the appendix.

*　　*　　*

We have had enough white for the moment: let us turn to blue, for in the first things of the year we shall find blue at its purest and most intense, echoing the keen, empty skies of March. Of all these blues, none—even from the hyacinth hosts—can rival the blue cowslip.

In his monumental work *The Amateur Gardener* Mr A. G. L. Hellyer observes that the blue cowslip: 'really has very little resemblance to a cowslip'. In most horticultural matters I kneel at Mr Hellyer's feet; he has long ago forgotten more about flowers than most of us could hope to learn in a hundred years. But in this matter of the blue cowslip, no. The blue cowslip *is* a cowslip. It is also, to our pain and grief, *Pulmonaria angustifolia*.

This is one of those flowers which, like the galtonia mentioned in the introduction, came to me late in life. Where had it been hiding all these years? I first saw it growing in a Sussex garden, on a morning of March. The brilliant blue of the flowers in the wintry sunlight recalled a passage in a picture by Monet. I asked my host what it was.

'But Beverley, you *must* know it. It's merely a blue edition of "Soldiers and Sailors".'

That rang a bell. 'Soldiers and Sailors', the humble plant so often found in old cottage gardens, with speckled, hairy leaves and flowers that never seem to be able to decide whether they want to be pink or blue, like certain liberal-minded young undergraduates of one's acquaintance.

'So it is,' I said. 'Soldiers and Sailors.' But this homely title gives but a faint idea of the blue variety—perhaps bluer than any flower in nature, bluer than gentians or anchusas, with the luminous quality of a stained glass window when the sun shines through.

This small treasure is very easy to grow. You can plant it

in semi-shade or full sun, on any sort of soil, and it is one of those rare plants that does not seem to mind having to compete with the roots of trees. My own cluster is right up against the trunk of an old pear.

For some obscure reason, many nurserymen do not stock it, maybe because they consider it 'common'. Those who list it are duly credited in the appendix.

*   *   *

Now that we are on the subject of blue, I should like to say a word about the blue polyanthus, which is a perfect foil for the blue cowslip.

This may strike some people as rather odd. Most of the writers on gardens do not agree that flowers gain in brilliance if they are placed in close proximity to other flowers of the same colour; the average herbaceous border is full of violent contrasts.

This has always seemed to me regrettable, particularly in flower arrangements. White lilies look best against a white wall in a white vase; if they are set against a dark background, as in most flower competitions, they lose much of the subtlety of their line and colour. The gold of daffodils is enhanced by the gold of forsythia. Green echoes green and complements it; the moss on the leeward side of a beech is all the more vivid because of the green shadows from the leaves above. Of all the colours that seems to demand the companionship of its own kind none clamours more loudly than red; you cannot go wrong when you bring reds together; and even a dark, demure rose like Guinee gains depth and intensity if you climb it up an old red brick wall.

So it is with the blues, and especially with the blue polyanthus in conjunction with other early blues. By the time these words are printed let us hope that these exquisite flowers will be more widely grown. Needless to say they are already established in the gardens of those who 'keep up with the time', but I make no apology for referring to them; many people who saw them in my garden last year had never encountered them before.

For the same reason there may be an excuse for assuming that the *Primula denticulata* is familiar to many amateur gardeners. To them, primulas are pretty little things growing in shady borders and by the side of streams, looking rather like primroses on stalks, and that is all there is to say about them.

But there is a great deal more to say about them.

My own *Primula denticulata*—open to inspection—grow to an average height of two feet, and when the flowers are over the plants are the size of cabbages. (Admittedly they get plenty of compost.) They flower, on and off, for ten weeks and they come in every shade of pale violet, pinkish mauve, pale blue and wistaria. There are also white varieties, but these have an unfortunate tendency to revert to type. I used to think that this was because the bees were always fussing and fuming round them, getting the pollen mixed up, but Mr Page informs me that the bees are not responsible. And what Mr Page says is good enough for me.

Some people—particularly some women—may not care for these shades of mauve and violet, which are surely among the loveliest colours of Nature, particularly when they are mingled with white and silver. Norman Hartnell once said that he has spent thirty years trying to make women wear them, without success. Women seem to have come to the conclusion that mauve does something unkind to their complexions. I trust that they will not allow this prejudice to extend to the garden.

But apart from *denticulata*, the modern primula is to be had in an astonishing range of colour—copper and wine-red and rose and butter-yellow with a silver undercoat. In my own garden, assisted by the aforesaid compost, they sometimes reach a height of four feet. There is no reason why they should not do the same in yours . . . provided that you will pay attention to the following words of warning.

First Word of Warning

Never put them in full sunlight. If you do, the leaves flop all over the place on the first warm day and look like dying cauliflowers. On the other hand, never plant them in full shade, or they will grow thin and spindly, and may not flower at all. This is the sort of gardening advice that always irritates me, because it sounds as though the writer assumed that every gardener has acres of varied site to choose from. Nevertheless I have to give it because it happens to be true.

Second—and Very Important—Word of Warning

After reading this chapter you may decide—and I hope you will—to invest in a packet of *Primula denticulata*. And you may write in early spring to some quite reputable firm, who will send you a packet of seed, which you will sow correctly, following all the directions. And nothing whatever in the way of primulas will happen. Weeds will happen, moss will happen, heartbreaks will happen—but no primulas.

What have you done wrong? Nothing. Then who is to blame? The firm who sold you the seeds. And this is where I feel that I really should wave an admonitory finger at some of those firms who sell seeds at the wrong time of the year. I have made fairly extensive experiments with primula seeds which prove that their period of viability is limited, at most, to six months, after which they are in no way reliable and often quite sterile. Which means, quite bluntly, that if you buy seeds in early spring you are buying stuff that is probably dead, and should, by rights, have been thrown on the rubbish heap.

If these words get me into bad odour with any of the big seed firms, I really cannot help it; the matter is too serious to be glossed over. Seeds are not immortal; some live longer than others, but none live for ever. The best results with primulas are obtained from seeds plucked straight from a living plant in June. You needn't worry about them not being ripe enough, for you can raise fine plants from seeds that are still quite green.

In short, never buy primula seeds later in the year than October, and sow them as soon as they arrive.

Primulata
pulverulenta

CHAPTER FOUR

A DIVERSITY OF DAFFODILS

IT would be untrue to suggest that the best gardeners are widely travelled; there are many humble but brilliant gardeners, working away in obscurity all over the country, who have never been able to afford even to cross the Channel.

I have often thought what fun it would be, if one were a millionaire, to give these men and women a chance to widen their horizons. To send them off to the Holy Land, in early spring, to feast their eyes on the clusters of wild irises that gather outside the village of Nazareth, shining in the grass like little pools that have fallen straight from heaven. To hang before them the dazzling tapestries of bougainvillaea, as it drapes the white walls of Tangier—so very different from the pale ghosts that shiver in the cool house at Kew, as the rain taps on the roof. To send them even further afield, so that they might marvel at the golden ferns of Trinidad— the only 22-carat gold in Nature; to fly over the turbulent golden seas of mimosa in Australia; to climb the mountains outside Darjeeling and suddenly, through a clearing, to glimpse a tree whose boughs seem laden with snow, but prove on closer inspection to be sheeted in white orchids.

However, one is not a millionaire, so that these philanthropic excursions must remain a pleasant dream. The humble gardeners of Britain must continue to work their miracles in the teeth of the brambles and the blizzards.

All the same, though travel may not be an essential to the gardener, it certainly puts ideas into one's head. Not till I was carried on a stretcher through the winding defiles of the North-West Frontier during the war did I realize, through a haze of morphia, the piercing beauty of the wild striped tulips nodding their heads in the wake of our melancholy cortege. I don't mean the Rembrandt tulips—which I grow in preference to almost every other variety—but the simpler and more primitive tulip *Tulipa stellata* which one sometimes sees in old Dutch flower paintings. It is white with a pink stripe; the white is as pure as the linen on the table of a Dutch housewife and the pink is as pretty as the colour in her cheeks. These tulips are hard to come by. You will not find them in the catalogues of any nurseryman; you have to 'know people' in order to get them—usually very peculiar people, too.

But the most startling floral discovery that came to me through travel was the winter daffodil, that flowers in November—the *Sternbergia lutea*.

Perhaps we should begin by observing that the sternbergia is not really a daffodil at all; why anybody should ever have described it as such is something of a mystery. In design and in colour it is almost indistinguishable from a yellow crocus, except that it is twice the size of a spring crocus and that the yellow has no touch of orange—it is butter yellow, flavoured with lemon. And it is very glistening.

I had known the sternbergia for many years and had grown it with varying success. Very varying. There had been one season when it was spectacular; planted on a slope in a tiny rockery its flames kept burning all through a still dry November, and were only quenched by torrential rains a few days before Christmas. They really were like flames, and as they shone in the sombre cheerless garden they put me in mind of candles that somebody has left burning in a deserted house.

But that only happened in one year. During most other seasons they sulked and spluttered, and sometimes they did not come up at all. My only consolation was that all one's most distinguished contemporaries seemed to be having the same trouble. They all described the sternbergia as so 'temperamental' that it was hardly worth growing.

And then, three years ago I went for the summer to Corfu, the island that lies like a painted ship off the barren hills of Greece, and that was the beginning of a love affair with the island. So much so, that I was back again in October, and it was here that the sternbergias came back into my life with a bang.

I had gone for a walk in the hills; the sun was low, the heat of the day was over, and the whole world seemed enveloped in a blue haze of enchantment. I struck off the road into an orchard of olive trees, scrambled up a little cliff and suddenly they were there before me—'a crowd, a host, of golden daffodils'. And I had a Mediterranean version of all the emotions that Wordsworth experienced when he saw the daffodils. (Though Dorothy Wordsworth happened to see them first—a fact which is not usually noted by literary historians.)

We will cut the ecstasies with a good honest word that I muttered to myself as I stood there on that little hill—the word drainage.

That was the heart of the matter—drainage. It stood out a

mile. For the sternbergias, as they cascaded over the rocks, were bold and brilliant. But as soon as the slope became less steep, they began to fade away, and when they reached the level, they stopped altogether. It was one of the most vivid object lessons in natural history that one could have had and —if I may look forward a moment—it was constantly repeated in the next few days, all over the island. On a steep slope—abundance; on the level—next to nothing. I even saw them growing, like wallflowers, on the crumbling bricks of a ruined house.

The non-gardener may think that this is much ado about nothing, but I hope that there may be some gardeners who will agree that these facts are worthy of record, particularly as I have since put them to a practical test with complete success.[1] This very beautiful flower should be far more widely seen in the winter garden; it lights the November days with a golden gleam that does not come again till the debut of the aconites in February. The reputation of temperamentality is undeserved, it is merely wrongly placed.

Drainage. If I write that word again, I shall begin to feel like that brilliant surgeon, the late Sir William Arbuthnot-Lane who believed, probably rightly, that most of the ills to which the flesh is heir are due to inadequate elimination. A woman once remarked to me at a cocktail party that he 'rushed round Mayfair cutting out people's colons as if he were pruning a privet hedge'. Well—Mayfair, and privet hedges, are none the worse for pruning.

PRACTICAL NOTE

Sternbergia lutea bulbs, at the time of writing, cost 8s. 6d.

---

[1] In a Somersetshire garden. My own is too flat.

a dozen. You can plant them at any time in the late summer. I won't go on about drainage, but I wouldn't dream of risking them on any level surface, and I would see that they had plenty of sand round the roots. They need every moment of sun that you can give them. Once established, they should never be moved.

Hoop petticoat daffodils (*Narcissus bulbocodium* and its varieties).

The hoop petticoat daffodils—six inches tall with flowers smaller than a thimble—might have been specially designed for 'shrinkers'. A 'shrinker', as I have explained in previous books, is a person who is able—well, simply to shrink. To reduce himself, mentally, to the size of the flower he is contemplating. To take a deep breath and swoop soilwards, so that he finds himself gazing into the multi-coloured dome of a fritillary as if he were contemplating the frescoes in the Sistine Chapel. To take a whole hour—in his mind—climbing precariously from the level of the lawn up the stern slopes of a suburban rockery, filled with awe and apprehension at the wild torrents of aubretias that may engulf him, and send him to an exquisite death in a maelstrom of mauve.

Shrinking, today, is an almost forgotten art. Which is almost certainly the principal reason for the ghastly state of the world we live in.

I first encountered the miniature daffodils, *en masse*, in Portugal. We were motoring through the mountains above Cintra and suddenly, after turning a sharp corner, we saw that somebody had obligingly draped the fields in cloth of gold. In England, of course, we would have registered 'buttercups' and passed on. But they could not possibly be buttercups, in these parts, at this time of the year. So we stopped the car and got out to investigate. And when we found that they were miniature daffodils, gave a deep sigh and sat down, in a sort of daze, on at least five pounds worth of *Narcissus bulbocodium conspicuus.*

It was a curious sensation, parking one's posterior on so precious a patch of blossom. They were growing so thickly that either one sat down on them or one did not sit down at all. So we sat down on them—though with a faint sense of guilt at the thought of the horror with which such conduct would be regarded at home.

And that brings me to perhaps the main problem of these little flowers when you introduce them into your own garden —where to plant them. They are so tiny that they can easily get lost, or trampled on, or forgotten when the spring has gone and the hosts of summer are on the march. It isn't a question of shade or sunshine, it is merely a matter of strategic position. Perhaps my own solution may give you some ideas. I have three groups. The first is planted in a pocket in the small square of crazy-paving outside my front door. Here, their gold shows up beautifully against the grey stone. The second group is at the foot of an old red brick pillar on which stands a porphyry urn. Nobody could possibly step on them in this position; they are in full sunshine and they seem to like the rather gritty soil in this part of the garden. And the third—to show how accommodating they are—is naturalized under the copper beech, planted in little pockets of loam to offset the greediness of the roots. Here, admittedly they sometimes give me qualms in case the wild grass swamps them. But so far they have survived, aided by a little tactful snipping round the stems with a pair of nail scissors.

So I think that these are flowers that you must have, whether your garden is great or small and whether you are a 'shrinker' or not. They may even teach you to become one by their annual reminder that beauty is not a question of size. And if you have no garden at all, you can still grow them very successfully in an earthenware pan in the back-yard.

PRACTICAL NOTE

You can spend as much as £10 a hundred on miniature daffodils, if you are the sort of person who goes to the Daffodil Show after luncheon, tingling with hock, and filled with a longing to get away from it all. But this is not really the best way to go about things. Far more sensible to go in the early morning, holding this list in your hand:

1. *Narcissus bulbocodium conspicuus.* Which is difficult enough to say, hock or no hock. This is the true hoop petticoat and will set you back 30s. a hundred.
2. *Narcissus asturiensis. (Syn. N. minimus.)* 45s. a hundred —presumably because it is smaller. Obviously, if you earn your living by being a dwarf, the dwarfer you are, the higher your fee. But there really isn't all that in it—a mere fraction of an inch. So unless you are a super-shrinker, I would settle for Number One, unless you choose . . .
3. *Narcissus triandrus albus.* 30s. a hundred, variety rather paler than the others. It has the charming sub-title Angels' Tears, and though it is about two inches taller than the others it is still very much a miniature.

CHAPTER FIVE

THE BEANSTALK TECHNIQUE

ALTHOUGH this is a book that can have no shape, as we have observed before, there may be a few who will read it as it is written, beginning at page one and ending—after a suitable allowance for skipping—at whatever the number of the last page may prove to be. I wish that I could provide a story-line for such indulgent folk, instead of dragging them here, there and everywhere into all these odd corners, asking them to look at this, that and the other.

However, this is not a book in which a story-line is really demanded. If it had been, there would have been no difficulty in contriving one. All that one would have needed to do would be to call the first chapter 'Things to Do in

January', and the last chapter 'Things to Do in December'. But I can think of so many non-horticultural things to do in both these months that my advice might have lacked conviction.

All the same, even though we do not tell a story we should, I think, remind ourselves from time to time of the small stage on which our little floral episodes are set. Which makes me flick back the pages to Chapter One, and quote my own words: 'Descriptions of flowers suspended, as it were, in space, are apt to be boring . . . I want a frame for the picture.'

So here, we will relax, step back, and study the picture through its frame. Or rather, through the garden door.

The first reaction of the average visitor, when he walks through that door—a small, faded green door, leading from Ham Common—is that he is entering a *mature* garden. Whether he likes it or not is neither here nor there—all I am claiming, at the moment, is that the general effect is one of a garden that has mellowed with age. 'But you must have been here for twenty years!'—that is a stock exclamation that I have heard at least a hundred times. And it is usually followed by suggestions to the effect that one's fingers must be exceptionally green or that one must have the secret of magic potions that make things grow like Jack's beanstalk.

The explanation is not so mysterious; it is contained in one word—rhododendrons. These are the shrubs, fully grown and planted in mass, which give the garden its illusion of maturity. Nothing else in nature could have done it. Rhododendrons can be transplanted with every hope of success when they have reached a size which, in the case of any other shrub, would make moving impractical. This is a simple piece of information which is, of course, elementary to the rhododendron expert, but is evidently unknown to the average amateur, judging by the questions which I am asked. Time and again people have stood in front of shrubs—some of them ten feet tall with a spread of a dozen feet—and exclaimed: 'But you can't have just put them in when they were this size!' Well, I did; and as I have observed before, they are open to inspection.

There is only one essential to this business of acquiring and transplanting full-grown rhododendrons; unless you are very rich you must first enlist the friendship and the services of an amiable millionaire. This will save everybody a great deal of trouble, with the possible exception of the millionaire. In my case the millionaire lived in Sussex, in an old house that had been a second home to me in my youth, surrounded by hundreds of acres of superb rhododendrons which were beginning to suffocate one another. (This is much the best sort of millionaire to choose.) I set out to persuade him that he would really be much happier—and so would the rhododendrons—if a couple of lorry-loads of them could be transferred to my patch, and after a short sharp campaign he heaved a deep sigh and agreed that I was probably right. And one day the lorries arrived, bearing their cargo of immense shrubs, which needed three men to lug them across the lawn. It seemed incredible that they should survive, but there has not been a single casualty.

Failing a millionaire—and I should be the first to admit that the finding and snaring of millionaires is not all that easy—you just have to grit your teeth, and tighten your belt, and buy them yourself. The important thing to remember is that it *can* be done. Indeed I have done it, when no millionaire was available. For example, one of my most beautiful rhododendrons is an eight-foot standard of the variety

Cynthia, which is a glowing pink fringed with carmine. I met it at one of the Chelsea shows where it was the pride and joy of a superb display, and I said to the man that I had to have it, and he said that it was not for sale, and I said that if he did not let me have it a curse would fall upon him, and upon his children, to the third and fourth generation. Finally, like the millionaire, he heaved a deep sigh and agreed that I was probably right.

The significance of all this will not be lost upon those who are not as young as they might be. One of the tragedies of life for those who love flowers, and who long to end their days in a garden of their own creating, is the fact that, only too often, it is almost too late to begin. By the time they have saved enough to retire and buy a little house and start to plan, the evenings are closing in on them. It is almost as though the shadow of Father Time were falling across the pages of the nurserymen's catalogue. This is where the brave and brilliant armies of the rhododendrons can come to their aid. And this is where I am suddenly seized by a feeling that perhaps my recommendations about the millionaire may have sounded rather heartless. They were not meant to be; they were really only variations on the theme that 'where there's a will there's a way'. For like those whom I have been addressing, my resources both in money and in time are not unlimited.

*　　*　　*

I am a sucker for rhododendrons and if I were limited to only one flower in the garden I should unhesitatingly choose them—for their grandeur and their delicacy; their fantastic range of colour, from almost black to glistening white; for their exquisite variety of design, from the clustering coral bells of Lady Chamberlain to the flamboyant trusses of Pink Pearl; for the many months in which they delight us, from early February, when the 'Praecox' opens its buds of palest mauve, to the dusty days of August when the branches of the Polar Bear are laden with scented snow. Even for their fragrance. One of my annual pilgrimages is to the cool house at Kew, to stand alone by the *Rhododendron 'Fragrantissimum'*, which fills the whole house with the perfume of frozen incense.

I am aware that some people do not 'get' them. Even as sensitive a spirit as John Betjeman once described them to me as a 'stockbrokers' flower'. If this is indeed the case, the stockbrokers are to be felicitated. But such a criticism, of course, could only come from one who associated them exclusively with the glossy, prosperous purlieus of outer London where neo-Tudor mansions smirk at their reflections in blue-tiled swimming-pools. One may not care for the neo-Tudor mansions any more than one cares for the gardens surrounding them, but that is scarcely a reason for condemning Tudor in its entirety. To cleanse one's mind of these prejudices it is not necessary to go to Thibet, where the rhododendrons march up the hillside like armies with banners; one need only take a bus to Windsor and walk through the fabulous Savill Gardens. And having done so, proceed with the savings of the children's money-boxes to one of the hundreds of nurseries scattered all over the country—or rather, all over those parts of the country which are not poisoned by chalk. Some of these nurseries are rather hard to come by, and finding them is quite an adventure. You will find one or two helpful suggestions in the appendix, but as a general rule it is wisest to confine your hunting to an area that is within reasonable distance of your own home.

Not for the first time I have the feeling of trying to write the Lord's Prayer on a sixpence. There are about seven hundred species of rhododendron; these species are being constantly extended in a bewildering variety of blossom and leaf, and in the service of this queen of shrubs there is a vast army of experts all over the world. My only justification for writing about them at all is the enthusiasm of the amateur who came to them, perforce, late in life. ('Perforce', because in all my previous gardens I was cursed with lime.) And because the amateur, by the very shrillness of his excitement, can sometimes make himself heard, however vulgarly, above the learned expositions of the expert.

And so, as an amateur with perhaps that extra ten per cent of knowledge, let me mention some of the things about rhododendrons which may not be generally known to other amateurs.

Firstly, their range of colour, beginning with the yellows. The expert will hardly thank me for reminding him of such species as *Rhododendron campylocarpum* or *Rhododendron lutescens*, but I feel justified in doing so because many people, on first meeting them in my own garden, could not believe that they were rhododendrons at all, merely because they *were* yellow. A good nurseryman should be able to supply at least a dozen yellow, ranging from palest primrose to rich apricot and sulphur. Nor will the expert thank me for calling attention to a rhododendron—Purple Splendour—which is so dark that in some lights it looks almost black, like certain pansies, with jet black markings on a ground of deep purple velvet. As for the pinks and reds, the range is literally inexhaustible; Roget's *Thesaurus* does not even begin to cover the hues of this multi-coloured palette. And what about the whites and the maroons and the purples and the blues?

With so many colours available innumerable combinations suggest themselves; even the common *Rhododendron ponticum*, if you plant a scarlet Britannia at its base, creates an exciting clash of floral argument. However, some people—even rhododendron lovers—seem to have a dislike for *ponticums*, which flow in purple torrents through many of our native valleys every spring. Personally, I find them very beautiful, especially when they are seen through the pale shadows of silver birches, with maybe a few scattered pools of bluebells at their feet. But, if you have only a limited space you will probably wish for something more uncommon, and so, in its place I would plant the variety called *Fastuosum flore pleno*, which might be described as the *ponticum's* rich relation. The flowers are larger and of a more delicate colour; the purple has been refined into an exquisite shade of violet. Although this rhododendron bears all the stamp of aristocracy it is incredibly tough—tougher even than its comparatively plebeian ancestor. It does not seem to be affected by the bitterest frost. You can plant it in full sunshine without any fear that the petals will scorch or wilt, which is more than can be said for many roses. Best of all, it will stand up to the fiercest gales; even in full exposure, during the tempestuous winter of 1962, my *Fastuosums* sustained no more damage than if they had been common laurels.

This brings me to the rhododendron's greatest enemy—indeed, to the supreme enemy of all growing things—wind. When the gales sweep across the common I lie in bed unable to sleep with a terrible feeling that I am being torn up by the roots. We can guard against the cold, we can defeat the drought, and we have at our disposal an armoury of weapons with which to wage war against the legions of the insect world. But the assaults of the wind are fierce and incessant, and launched with a deadly cunning. Even in a garden like my own, surrounded by high walls, the wind sweeps in, tearing at the shrubs with icy fingers as though our efforts to combat it had charged it with an extra malice. Walls, indeed, offer only a very limited protection; the wind seems to swirl round them, like waves over a breakwater. The only sure shield is afforded by ancient trees towering high above them, bearing the main impact of the attack. And these, let's face it, most of us have not got.

However, I have my big copper beech, and the walnut, and a few gnarled old fruit trees, and round these the more delicate rhododendrons are disposed as artfully as we can manage. You would be surprised at the amount of wind protection that is given by *open* branches; a well-grown twiggy shrub like a deutzia, for example, is more helpful than a brick wall. And in each of the four corners there is some special treasure. In one of them there is my Lady Chamberlain. It may sound affected to describe this as a carillon in coral, but I can think of no other metaphor, for the branches are thickly hung with coral bells which seem, when the wind touches them, to be making music. In another corner there is my *falconeri*, whose immense leaves are thickly clustered, on the inner side, with bronze. In yet another corner is my tree rhododendron, *arboreum*, which I bought when it was twenty feet tall and—to be frank—have never ceased to regret. For though it is still alive, it does not look happy and it has yet to flower. The most sheltered corner of all, protected on all sides, is reserved for the fabulous Polar Bear, which produces its large snow white flowers, that are scented as sweetly as gardenias, in mid-September.

Not a collection, I should be the first to agree, that would excite the experts—nothing that would cause any great sensation at Kew. Merely a small treasury of beauty that has been gathered together in a little time, with a lot of love and more than a fair share of luck. And as such, maybe, worthy of consideration.

Apart from their glittering gifts of colour and form, rhododendrons have another supreme merit; they require practically no attention. Once you have found the right position for them all that they need, apart from watering and an annual mulch, is to have the dead blossoms nipped off. And even this is not absolutely vital, because obviously, such a procedure would be impossible in an ancient garden stocked with fully grown specimens. The only reason for dead-heading is to stimulate growth. Of all the chores in the garden I find this the most agreeable. I use a safety razor and slice each flower very carefully just above the little fresh green shoots that will form the branches for next year's flowers. And I let the blossoms tumble to the earth so that they form a glowing pool of colour which makes them look, from a distance, as though Monet had been wandering around with a loaded brush.

Watering, of course, is of great importance and here I would suggest a cheap and simple device which I have not seen employed elsewhere. Although there are many sprinklers on the market I know of none which really simulates natural rain, which is, of course, what they would like best, for they absorb moisture through the leaves. (The reason why they curl in their leaves during very cold weather is to retain this moisture.) So we take a hollow brass rod, cut to about eight feet, and a length of plastic hose, into one end of which we have pushed an ordinary cheap sprinkler such as one sticks into the lawn—not the sort which whirls round and startles the cats. Then all we have to do is to fix the sprinkler to one end of the hose and the other end to a garden tap, turn on the water, and that is that. To listen to one's own rain pattering on to the thirsty leaves gives one an almost god-like sensation . . . except, of course, when one is not quite sure whether one may not be contravening some regulation of the water board.

So ends my small celebration of a great subject. I shall send a copy of it to John Betjeman.

*　　*　　*

A few moments ago we mentioned Kew, and this prompts me to tell of an occasion when my garden did in fact attract the attention of this venerable establishment. For here is another example of the fact that Jack's beanstalk is not an entirely mythical tree, but can in fact be made to flourish within twenty miles of London.

The beanstalk in question is a eucalyptus of the species called *cordata* and it came into my life by one of those charming accidents with which every gardener is familiar. I had been motoring in darkest Kent, with a vague idea of seeing gardens, visiting nurseries, and gazing over other people's hedges, which is always a rewarding way of adding to one's stock of knowledge. On the way home I got lost, and decided to turn back. So I reversed into a rutted lane which looked as though it led to a deserted farmyard, and suddenly I saw a small notice announcing in faded and almost illegible letters that this was the entrance to X's nurseries. This seemed, to say the least of it, unlikely, for any introduction less calculated to attract the general public could hardly be imagined. However, I decided to investigate, and drove in. As the car bumped and groaned up the muddy hill I realized that here was a realm of enchantment; as far as the eye could see there were drifts of rhododendrons—avenues and terraces of rhododendrons, azaleas, and a bewildering variety of flowering shrubs. Afterwards I was to learn that X's nurseries are in fact famous all over the world; this was merely their way of doing business. They just didn't greatly care for advertising and they were not interested in trippers. It was rather as though the proprietor of the greatest restaurant in Paris should decide, in a moment of whimsy, that the most suitable entrée to his establishment was through the Flea Market.

At the top of the hill there were some buildings with nobody in them. Long experience has taught me that there never *is* anybody in buildings at nurseries; one trudges about for twenty minutes before discovering a youth who tells one that one wants to see Mr Wilkins, which is all too true, one wants to see anybody at all—but how? Mr Wilkins was last seen, apparently, in the conifer section, so off one trudges for at least a mile, only to be told that he has taken refuge in the cold greenhouses. So it was on this occasion. It was a long time before I discovered our Mr Wilkins, though that was not his name, but he was worth waiting for; he proved to be a man of seemingly inexhaustible erudition. And in spite of his other-worldly appearance—he looked as if he had wandered out of an amateur production of *A Midsummer Night's Dream*—he must have been an excellent salesman, for when I left I had given so large an order for rhododendrons, azaleas, camellias and various other delights that I felt somewhat pensive on the way home.

But had I *really* ordered a collection of a dozen eucalyptus trees? That was the question I asked myself a few weeks later, when they were delivered, looking very pale and forlorn, with the sacking round their roots. Surely there must be some mistake? However, I could not be sure, because I had been in a sort of daze throughout my visit to X's, and in any case I had not the heart to query the consignment, because of the pleasure which it gave to Page, who is always delighted when he is presented with something rare and exotic.

So in they went. And though it would be an exaggeration to say that they started to grow as soon as they were planted, they all flourished exceedingly, helped by a succession of mild winters. But none grew with a more beanstalk speed than the *cordata*.

*   *   *

The clock switches forward three years and three months, to a bleak afternoon in November. Spotlit in the middle of the stage, or rather in the shadow of the tool-shed, stands the *cordata*, looking as pretty as anything you ever saw in any pantomime. Eighteen feet tall, with leaves of palest grey, covered with creamy flowers—there must be several hundreds of them—shaped like miniature powder-puffs. One or two bewildered and obviously misguided bees are sticking their noses into them, and reeling away, wondering if summer has come again.

Underneath this phenomenon, flanked by Page and my-self stands Mr Souster, who is curator of the Temperate House at Kew. We had written to him because we really did feel that we had stumbled, by chance, on to something rather exceptional, and he whole-heartedly endorsed this view. He had never before encountered the *cordata* flourishing out of doors in this part of the world—nor, indeed, several of the other varieties—and when he left he gave us the distinct

73

impression that we had caused him to revise his previous opinions as to their hardiness, we felt that this, coming from Kew, was a nice feather in our caps.

I hope that Mr Souster will not mind being quoted in evidence, for I should like to make England eucalyptus-conscious. This great and noble family of trees is among the most rewarding in Nature. Perhaps you must see them in their own countries to realize their full splendour. I first fell in love with them in Australia, when I went there as a young man with Melba, and maybe it is for this reason that I associate them with music, as though a silver voice were stealing through the branches. And certainly they make the sweetest music on the southern winds, when their leaves are an exquisite foil to the golden plumes of the mimosa. Later I was to meet them in New Delhi (where in winter the cold is as acute as in many parts of England). There they were planted as thickly as coppices of silver birch, of which, pictorially, they are a sort of exotic variation. And again—like thousands of other tourists—I have motored through long avenues of them in the mountains of Portugal, where they attain to fabulous heights, and where the shadows they cast are so deep and yet so luminous that the wild scillas below them seem to be tinged with a spectral shade of green.

I mention these three localities not merely in order to paint pretty pictures but because they may be of some botanical significance. No conditions could offer sharper contrasts than Australia, India and Portugal. In Australia they had to endure long periods of drought, but they were never subject to severe cold. In India, on the other hand, they had to face bitter frosts. In Portugal they had neither great cold nor great heat, but long periods of drenching rain. Yet in all these places they flourished exceedingly. What are we to make of this problem? I think we may find at least a partial answer by stating the one ordeal that they were *not* required to endure in any of these places—wind, which once again discloses itself as the gardener's greatest enemy. They never grew on the fringes of woods, only in the deep sheltered interiors, and they were never seen on the windward side of mountains.

Postscript

I add this note with sorrow but by no means with despair. Since writing the foregoing chapter we have suffered one of the harshest winters within living memory. The weather has made headline news. For days on end the wind has been at full gale force; the thermometer has sunk to record depths, and stayed there; as if this were not enough, there have been constant heavy falls of snow. Even the hollies and the laurels have been battered. It is hardly surprising, therefore, that the eucalyptus trees are looking exceedingly sorry for themselves, with the delicate leaves frost burnt as though by fire, and some of the slender branches snapped right off. But they are still alive . . . just; when one goes out to scrape the bark with icy fingers, one discovers that the sap is green and vivid. And even if they die I shall still feel grateful to them; they have been an enchantment for three glorious years. So I shall continue to sing their praises in the hope that the song will not prove to be an elegy.

PRACTICAL NOTE

For those who have neither the time nor money to go to X's—in any case, they would probably lose themselves—the cheapest and simplest way to make the great eucalyptus experiment is to buy seeds which, somewhat to my surprise, are available at upwards of a shilling a packet. Apart from the *cordata*, the species which are regarded as the hardiest are *gunnii*, the cider gum, and *urnigera*, which has apple green leaves, and comes from Tasmania. The seeds germinate like mustard and cress, and the growth, per annum, is approximately six feet.

Sternbergia lutea

Tropaeolum speciosum

Ilex aquifolium

Kalmia latifolia

CHAPTER SIX

MYSTERIES

So far, everything seems to have gone very well. Almost irritatingly well, perhaps, for the average gardener. That is the trouble with so many books of this nature; the authors so seldom confess to their failures. As a result, their gardens do not really come to life; they have an almost dream-like quality in which the lawns are like softly-lit stages and the flowers dance in the borders like a well-drilled chorus.

So this might well be a suitable moment for pausing to consider some of the things that have gone wrong—not only in my present garden but throughout my gardening career—and how sometimes, but by no means always, to

77

put them right.

Which brings us to Elinor Glyn.

Once, as a very young man, I was walking across the lawn of a country house with that remarkable lady when she suddenly stopped, closed her eyes, and put her hand on her forehead. For a moment I thought she had been taken queer, but the tension was relieved a moment later when she nodded, smiled in her most sphinx-like manner, and murmured: 'Clay! I knew it. Thick blue clay!'

As we resumed our promenade she explained that on thick blue clay she was always ill at ease, and that she had been feeling ill at ease ever since luncheon. So, as it happened, had I, but I had attributed it to the game pie. However, there seemed no reason to doubt her sincerity, for her whole life and conduct was ruled by these strange psychic influences. She had already told me, for example, that she could not possibly sleep in any bed where her head was not pointing directly to the magnetic north, and when I asked her if she therefore travelled with a compass she replied, no, it was not necessary, she always knew by instinct. If her head was not due north, she either shifted around, or turned the bed, or moved to another room. I remember thinking that this must have made any form of passionate exercise somewhat complicated.

Nor do I see any reason to question the authenticity of her reaction to the soil which—so she told me—was so sharp and clear that, even if she were blindfold, she could instantly tell whether she was standing on clay or chalk or sand or peat. She turned and fixed me with her brilliant green eyes. 'I am a peat person,' she said. 'And so are you.' She spoke truly, and I only wish that I had realized the significance of her diagnosis; it would have saved me a great deal of time and money in my gardening career.

For each of us has his special soil, to which he 'vibrates'—for lack of a better word—in harmony or in discord, and the more sensitive the spirit, the more marked the vibration. Emily Brontë, for example, was so essentially a 'peat person' that away from her moors and her heathers she languished. John Betjeman, on the contrary, is a chalk person—he marches with the Wiltshire downs and his eye is on the white horses carved on the distant hill; not for him the wind on the heath, brother, he hears sweeter music when it blows through a hedge of stunted hawthorn.

And there are clay persons, quite obviously, such as Mr Graham Greene, very heavy clay indeed.

*　　*　　*

It was because I did not know, right at the beginning of my career, whether I was a peat person or a sand person or a clay person or a chalk person, that I suffered many heart-breaking disappointments, and one of the purposes of this book is to save you these same disappointments. You *must* consider your soil; its nature and quality are so vital that I make no apology for asking you to regard it in the light in which I suggested, as something with almost mystic qualities. One of the few criticisms to be made of the honourable company of British nurserymen is that they do not always emphasize this point to their customers. In the first garden I ever owned, of which I wrote in *Down the Garden Path*, I had extensive dealings with a firm of nurserymen who were fully acquainted with the nature of my soil, what it could grow and what it could not. And when, in ignorance, I sent in large and expensive orders for shrubs which would assuredly die in it, they should have queried these orders, and given a little friendly advice. They did no such thing. They sent along the shrubs and pocketed their profit, and the shrubs, of course, promptly gave up the ghost. This was very naughty of the nurserymen. Their behaviour was on a par with that of a doctor who allows a patient to drink himself to death because he has shares in the local pub.

However, such cases are few and far between. And if gardeners would only take the trouble to *read* their catalogues —some of the British catalogues are written in admirable prose, clean and terse and pungent—they would reduce their failures by fifty per cent.

And yet, even when one has followed all the 'directions on the packet', even when one has had the soil sifted and analysed and has gone to endless trouble to repair its deficiencies, if any, the result may be a gloomy failure. Why? What is the explanation of the mystery? Why, for example, have I never been able to grow a kalmia? This is surely one of the most beautiful shrubs in Nature, with leaves like a myrtle, and tiny waxen flowers, not unlike a pink lily of the valley, gathered together in closely packed trusses. They would look exquisite under a glass case on a Victorian mantlepiece. Well, I have followed kalmias all over the world. I have seen them rioting away in New England, grown in full sun, and subjected to a ferocity of frost from which we are mercifully spared. I have seen them flourishing in deep shade in the woods of Southern Ireland, almost sunless and perpetually damp. Nearer at home, I have met them exulting in sheer sand, wind-swept and sun-scorched. In all these cases the soil, admittedly, was acid, but none of the other conditions was alike. I have planted them in *all* these circumstances, and in one case I even went so far as to import a small mountain of sand, especially for their delectation. Always, they died, as though I had cast an evil spell over them. Not at once—just a slow lingering away, like a child that has lost the will to live. These are obviously flowers who do not like my wave-length. It is a comforting excuse when things go wrong, though I doubt whether you will find it mentioned in the proceedings of the Royal Horticultural Society.

*   *   *

To some people, no doubt, the idea that there may be a mystical element in the art of horticulture would be sheer nonsense; the average orthodox gardener would react as strongly against it as would the average doctor were you to ask his opinion of spirit-healing. Having witnessed some of the miracles of spirit-healing I am not unduly impressed by the orthodox reactions in either field. For I do indeed believe that flowers have feelings, and that these feelings extend to the human beings who tend them. If it is true—as it surely is— that there are 'green fingers', to which flowers react in sympathy, why should there not also be 'black fingers', from which flowers—certain flowers—withdraw in distaste?

By no other theory can I explain, for example, my own total failure to grow alstroemerias, the lovely Peruvian lilies that flower in July. On the packet—or rather on the bulb bag —it tells you that they 'resent lime'. Not a speck of lime did they get. It wasn't lime they resented, it was me. Again it said that they 'succeed best in half shade'. They got it, but they didn't succeed; my own shadow had fallen across them. In desperation I bought them in pots, and planted them already 'established'. But they died down and never came up again. 'Death,' they had obviously said to themselves, 'is better than the thought of seeing *that* face again.'

I can only assume that in some distant incarnation I had been cast in the role of a wire-worm, and that their delicate sensitivities had warned them that they were in the presence of an enemy.

*   *   *

One of these mysteries still plagues me—the Mystery of the Climbing Flame Nasturtium (*Tropaeolum speciosum*).

Anybody who has ever seen this lovely thing climbing up a wall or threading its delicate tendrils against the dark background of an old yew will certainly agree that it is very aptly named. Although the flowers are only half the size of the ordinary nasturtium, they are so bright that they give the effect of tiny flames licking the leaves—which in themselves are exquisitely shaped, like five-leaved clovers. And this effect of living fire is enhanced by the fact that this is a plant that flowers only in deep shade, so that the flames seem to be leaping in the dark.

But why did we speak of 'mystery'? Because this nasturtium stubbornly refuses to produce even the faintest flicker for hundreds of gardeners who grow it, or try to grow it, in seemingly ideal conditions. A while ago I was gardening correspondent for a Sunday newspaper, and I wrote an article about it. My title for the article was 'Flowering Flames', but the sub-editor—who had apparently been engaged for the sole purpose of slashing his pencil through anything that could conceivably be interpreted as 'Nichols' Whimsy'—decided that it would have more appeal if it was headed 'Don't Give This Plant to Junior'. A decision which made me purse my lips, ever so slightly.

However, perhaps the sub-editor was right. Quite evidently, as I was to learn a year later, this was *not* a plant that you should recommend to Junior—nor to most seniors. For weeks my mail-bag was filled with indignant letters from readers protesting that their flame nasturtiums hadn't come up. Or having come up, had merely spluttered and put their tongues out, prior to expiring. The tone of these letters was sometimes so acid that I took to replying in kind, until reprimanded by the sub-editor, who pointed out that such conduct was bad for circulation.

To compensate for this avalanche of abuse there were about fifty letters from readers thanking me for introducing them to a flower which, as one of them put it, was 'like a necklace of rubies hanging on a nail in my back-yard'. Note the word 'back-yard'; it emphasizes the fact that this is something that you can grow in the city. All it needs is a trellis for support, which it will begin to climb as soon as it shows itself above the ground in the middle of May. It dies down completely with the frosts, but comes up stronger than ever in succeeding years.

And now for the pay-off line. My own flame nasturtiums have completely disappeared. It is almost as though they flew away in the middle of the night. Moreover, in the two succeeding years in which I planted them, nothing whatever has happened. The same soil, the same positions, the same climatic conditions, the same everything. Result, nothing.

All the same, I shall go on trying. And I hope that you will try too, for you may be one of the fortunate few who are on the same psychic wave-length.

After this, it may seem faintly ironic to write the customary Practical Note. But when I *did* succeed with it, in those three happy years, it was by obeying one vital requirement—a long cool root run. This means precisely what it says; 'long', at least four feet of friable soil; 'cool', untouched by any but the faintest gleams of morning sunlight.

All for 1s. 6d. a packet. Sordid commercial details in the appendix. Please don't blame me if for some reason or other the flame nasturtium decides that your fingers are black.

*   *   *

I hope that I have written enough to dispel any illusion that mine is a garden where nothing ever goes wrong. Things constantly go wrong. And though I have suggested in all seriousness that sometimes the cause of these failures may not always be entirely material, obviously, in the great majority of cases they had a simple botanical explanation. Most of the failures in the garden, which appear so mysterious to the beginner, are the result of mere ignorance.

Ignorance, for example, of sex.

Sex, fortunately, does not often rear its ugly head in the garden. The birds and the bees go about their business—the birds spreading the seeds of the mistletoes and the bees making their discreet introductions of blossom to blossom in a golden trail of pollen. But sometimes, willy-nilly, the gardener must take sex into account. As in the case of the holly.

The sexual proclivities of the holly, particularly the lovely variegated gold and silvers, are remarkable, and suggest that they should be made the subject of an inquiry by a sort of horticultural Wolfenden Committee. For example, if you bought a Golden Queen and a Silver Queen you would naturally expect that they would at least have feminine tendencies. But no—both are firmly male.

Golden King, on the other hand, is female. Curiouser and curiouser. Who thinks these names up?

As if this were not enough, the lovely common holly which we find all over Britain in the hedgerows is, in a manner of speaking, trisexual. That is to say, it may be either male, female, or very occasionally bisexual. So until you see it actually producing its berries, you hardly know whether to address it as Sir, Madam or It.

What are we to do in all this tangle? To be absolutely on the safe side, buy one of the common hollies that is already in berry and plant it in the neighbourhood of one of the male variegated varieties such as Silver Queen. Your common holly will then be assured of male company for the rest of its life.

The name of the common holly is *Ilex aquifolium,* and there is also a very gay variety with bright yellow berries. Choosing hollies is rather a tricky business, which demands more than the usual co-operation between buyer and seller. I would therefore suggest that a personal visit to the nursery will save a great deal of frustration and misunderstanding.

Green Dragon

Lilium candidum

CHAPTER SEVEN

CONSIDER THE LILIES

THERE has been enough talk of mystery and enough of failure, too, so let us return to the sunlight, and to success, and consider the lilies.

Though even here, in the case of one lily, the exquisite golden lily of Japan, *Lilium auratum*, there has been plenty of cause for gloom, not only in my own garden, but in thousands of gardens all over England and America. It is said to arise from a virus which causes them either to disappear completely or to come up on sickly yellow stems that rot away before the blossom has opened. If this sort of thing goes on some of us will soon feel tempted to follow the example of the

Japanese, who boil the bulbs and eat them like potatoes.

Page is inclined to put it all down to the atom bomb—one of the greatest lily farms of pre-war days was within a few miles of Hiroshima—and why should that idea be so ridiculous? Even on human beings the effects of radiation are little known; on plants there has been a minimum of research. If a team of botanists and physicists were jointly to examine some of the strange goings-on in the gardens of the world, it is possible that they might reach some disturbing conclusions.

However, we did not set out to make anybody's flesh creep, and the *auratum* is more affected than any other lily by this mysterious malaise. The rest of the great lily family is marching on from triumph to triumph. The modern lily is really 'going places', and one has to be very much on one's toes to keep up with it. What follows may help you to do so.

If I were asked to name the most beautiful flower in the world I would unhesitatingly choose one which few people in this country have ever seen, the Green Dragon lily. In America it is rather better known, for that is where it originated—in the Oregon lily farm of Jan de Graaf, two hundred miles west of the windy city of Chicago. But even in America, it is not sung or celebrated as it should be; there are no pilgrimages to Oregon, and nobody as yet has suggested setting up a statue of Mr de Graaf next to, and slightly larger than, the Statue of Liberty.

After this, you will not be surprised if my description of this flower is more than faintly ecstatic. Here goes. The Green Dragon is a *regale* lily powdered with the dust of emeralds, flowering by moonlight in a green glade. In case that sounds to you a bit thick—and on reading it over, that is rather how it sounds to me—I can only apologize. In shape and in scent it is the replica of a *regale*, except that the inner cup is of a more luminous gold. It is on the *outside* of the flower that green fingers have been straying, leaving this pale sheen of cool green. A plague on these descriptions—but how else can one make the flower blossom before you?

To try again—imagine that by some exotic process a wizard has contrived to blend ivory with jade. And that from this substance a great craftsman has carved . . . but no. We give up. Let's just call it an exceptionally fine *regale* tinted with a luminous green.

*   *   *

I have let myself go on the Green Dragon because by an exquisite fraction it is one degree more beautiful than its two brothers, Limelight, which has a distinct tinge of yellow, and Emerald Strain. And, maybe, rather more sweetly scented.

But these three lilies are expensive. Indeed, *all* lilies are expensive. So where do we go from here? Where do we go if we are really serious about this lily business, and if we want to bring into our gardens some of the members of this glittering host?

The answer—which will not appeal to teenagers—is that we grow them from seed.

And here, to my relief as much as yours, we can revert to the strictly practical.

There is nothing in the least esoteric about growing lilies from seed; they are as easy as mustard and cress. However, here is one tip which will make the whole thing more rewarding. Begin by buying two or three bulbs—though even a single bulb would do—and grow your seeds from the pods that the flowers produce. You will lose a year—what is a year between friends?—but you will be sure that your seeds are fresh and perfect, and all the time that they are growing you will have in your mind a clear picture of the loveliness that they are preparing for you, line by lovely line.

Gather the seeds when the pods are beginning to open, just before they are ready to fall on the summer soil. They should be ripe enough to tumble into the palm of your hand as soon as you shake the pods. Sow them in boxes in sandy loam, and give them a little counterpane of earth about a quarter of an inch thick. Set them in a corner of the garden where they won't be either scorched or sun-starved and don't let them get too dry. Bring them into the cool green-house when the cold weather starts, or, if you haven't such a convenience, put them on the window-sill of a cool room. They need hardly any watering in such conditions.

That is the drill for the first year. It is not very exciting. The real thrills begin in the following March, when the lilies begin to push through the earth wearing their seeds on top of their heads, like little hats. They grow swiftly all through the following weeks, and as soon as the second leaf appears you can prick them out into small pots. I like the modern pots of soluble compost which melt into the ground when you plant them in the open in the following spring. Then there is only one more year to wait before they flower. With any luck, they will go on flowering till the end of time —my time, at any rate, and probably yours. Unless, of course, somebody invents that wonderful pill of immortality which we all dream about. Everybody else, naturally, will have to die but not, surely, oneself? As Ivor Novello once said to me, lying in his bedroom at Redroofs, with the wide window that looked out on the lilacs of which he sang so sweetly.

Practicality, once again, seems to have evaded us. But lilies are so beautiful that surely no excuse is needed for asking you to remember that growing them from seed is 'as easy as mustard and cress'. Admittedly, they will not always 'come true'—this applies particularly to the hybrids, in which the green varieties must be classed—but does that matter so much? They will always 'come beautiful'.

A final word about growing things from seed, and the philosophy—or if that is too pompous a word—the mentality behind it.

The older a gardener gets, the more he is inclined to this method of propagation whenever it is possible. When I was very young I would have none of it—there seemed so brief a time ahead—unless one bought trees and planted them when they were at least six foot high, one would be a senile old gentleman of twenty-eight before they looked like trees at all.

Today, all that has changed. The time ahead has perceptibly shortened, but my patience has lengthened out. It is no longer necessary to buy tall trees, nor to choose them merely because they are quick growers. It does not seem to matter. So little, indeed, that last autumn I planted a tulip tree that almost certainly will not flower for thirty years, by which time . . . never mind. It would be a nice flower for somebody to set on a grave.

It is the same with bulbs and corms and roots and such like. My first asparagus bed was planted with three-year-old roots—to buy roots that were only two years was unthinkable; before one could pick a bunch one would be dead or stricken with the palsy, or in the middle of a war. (The latter possibility, one must admit, is perennially with us.) As for lilies or daffodils, or anything in that line—grow them from *seed*? Be your age, my dear chap! Well, at last I am endeavouring to be it.

*   *   *

A Note on the Arrangement of Lilies for the House

In another book of mine, called *Merry Hall*, which some people may still remember, I invented a character called Our Rose, who was a composite figure inspired by some of those professional floral decorators who spend their lives torturing flowers into patterns and positions which are an affront to Nature. I have never met any of these ladies in the flesh, and I doubt if I could tell you their names; for though their creations are to be seen in a thousand exhibitions they seldom run the risk of committing themselves to print. And yet, they have formed so vivid a composite picture in my mind that Our Rose, to me, is a living, breathing person. Breathing, indeed, rather heavily.

I have only seen one concoction in which Our Rose employed her fatal talents in the arrangement of lilies, and it was enough to turn the stomach. She used three dozen *regales*. Of these, the stems of one dozen had been plunged into red ink and allowed to soak, so that the lovely petals were finished with an unnatural glow, like rouge on the face of a choir-boy. Another dozen had been plunged into green ink, with the result that they resembled the cheeks of a corpse. The other dozen, oddly enough, had been left alone, presumably because she had run out of coloured inks.

These tortured blossoms were crucified on pinholders—sometimes one feels that Our Rose must have been born with a silver pinholder in her mouth, or somewhere or other—and transported to a very grand exhibition where they gained a first prize. To make the whole squalid story even more scarifying she had given her arrangement the title, 'Neapolitan Ice'.

I wish that Our Rose would divert her energy exclusively to the kitchen garden. I have never yet eaten asparagus from a pinholder, but I am quite willing to try.

But this little postscript was intended to be practical. What do we do with our lilies—if and when we pick them?

My own feeling is that as far as possible we leave them alone. We do not force them to fan out at unnatural angles, as is the practice of Our Rose and her sisters. Nor do we make a floral pyramid of them, cutting some of the stems so short that the petals only just manage to peer over the rim of the bowl—another favourite Rosean device. Nor do we stick a ghastly little figure at their base—usually described in Rosean circles as a 'figurine'. The use of a 'figurine' to complement a flower arrangement—whether it is a Disney lamb or a plastic gnome or a Dresden china shepherdess or even a painted Madonna—is the sign of a very vulgar mind. Who ever heard of any of the great masters, from Fantin-Latour, cluttering up a picture with a 'figurine'?

There are only two rules that I would make about arranging them, though 'rule' is perhaps too arbitrary a word. The first is that you should dispose them so that they do not look 'arranged' at all. None of that cruel lopping and twisting and contorting. The second is that you echo the colour of the flowers by the background against which you set them. White lilies, it is true, look very spectacular against a black screen, but they look far more beautiful against a white wall. And if you can set them in a gilt container, such as my old Regency wine-cooler, or a white urn flecked with gold, the two golds of the container and the pollen-dusted petals enhance each other's brilliance. If this sounds ultra-perfectionist there is nothing wrong with a plain glass jug.

PRACTICAL NOTE

There are a very large number of lilies which can be grown from seed, and though I prefer the method which I have advocated—buying your own bulbs, collecting your own seed from them when they flower the following year and sowing it immediately it is ripe—you can have every chance of success with fifty varieties which are readily available on the commercial market at a top price of 2s. 6d. a packet. These include many exciting hybrids. The Green Dragons and the other greens, unfortunately, are not available in this form and I must repeat my warning that even if you sow seed from one of your own flowers it may not come true to type. Let us therefore hope that the bulbs will shortly come down in price; at the time of writing the Green Dragons are about 30s. a bulb and the other greens about 7s. 6d.

CHAPTER EIGHT

CONSTANCE

AS YOU will have gathered, if you have accompanied me thus far in our journey down the garden path, I am very fond of arranging flowers and I have no great admiration for most of the professional ladies who arrange them.

But there was one woman whose way with flowers was so unique, whose whole approach to this enchanting domestic art was so fresh and creative, that she stands far apart from her tiresome imitators, and far, far above them. Her name, as you may have guessed, was Constance Spry, and this might be a fitting place in which to pay her tribute.

A hundred years hence the name of Constance Spry may

well have the same sort of lustre as the names of Gertrude Jekyll and Mrs Beeton. She was a woman destined for immortality in the Temple of the Household Gods. She has had the same sort of impact in her small and delightful world as many great reformers in a wider sphere, in the sense that we can speak quite definitely of a pre-Spry and a post-Spry period. When Constance first went out into the country lanes and gathered her faded leaves and her curious berries and her spectral branches, and when she proceeded to create from these unfamiliar ingredients designs of baroque beauty, she was writing a fragrant page of history. Needless to say she was imitated, she was misunderstood, she was parodied and sometimes she was abused. But she had established a point of no return; with Constance the art of flower decoration became adult, and nothing will ever be quite the same again.

I was honoured with the friendship of this charming person, who once paid me in one of her books the supreme compliment of saying that I was the only person she had ever met who had discovered a way of arranging sweet peas. If this seems a trivial matter to you, it does not seem so to me; often at times when the critics have been particularly beastly, I have retreated to a dark corner, and muttered to myself: 'Well, whatever they may say in the *Sunday Express*, at least Constance thought I could arrange sweet peas.'

The particular decoration to which she referred was at a party given in her honour. There were, of course, lilies in abundance, and vast vases in the Spry tradition, vases recalling the lines of the poet:

Voici des fruits, des fleurs, des feuilles et des branches,
Et puis, voici mon cœur, qui ne bat que pour vous.

95

But I wanted something of my very own, something which she could not accuse me of having copied from her. So I went out into the kitchen garden to think, and there I saw a long row of sweet peas. But what could one do with sweet peas?

This is what I did. I picked a bunch starting with the pure whites, and going on to the ivories and the creams, set them next to the very soft pinks, and the palest blues, followed by the cherries and the brighter blues, merging into the deep reds and the deepest blues, and ending with the dark violets and the near-blacks. I set these, in precisely that order, in a white basket. The result was a floral rainbow which made the party. And gave me, in the words of Constance Spry, my little accolade of immortality.

Here is a picture of her. She was intensely feminine, short and indeed rather dumpy, with bright eyes and a very clear, clean complexion. She was almost painfully sensitive because she always had an extraordinary illusion that she might be boring people when, in fact, she was bewitching them. When she forgot to be nervous she lit up and twinkled all over so that you felt she was dressed in sequins. She had a gentle, musical voice and very pretty hands. Oddly enough, she had a spark of naughtiness—as though she had sometimes lingered outside the dining-room door to listen to the gentlemen when they were letting their hair down over the port.

She lived in what appeared to me to be quite indescribable chaos. Obviously, it could not have been anything of the sort, but that was how it seemed to the outsider. For Constance, besides being a devoted wife and mother, apart from running a large business, supervising a restaurant, writing quantities of books and going to the ends of the earth to lecture, usually out of sheer good nature . . . Constance, in addition, presided as a sort of amiable queen bee over a large Establishment for Young Ladies. I do not know how many there were, but they swarmed all over her fantastically complicated premises, learning how to make omelettes, how to curtsey, how to arrange flowers, how to give parties, how to dress, and how to poke a cod in the stomach to see if it is fresh. To attempt to instruct even one young lady in such a repertoire would drive most women to a nervous breakdown, but Constance took it all in her stride. The young ladies came to her, often enough, as rather tiresome debutantes who could not boil an egg; they left her as brisk, efficient young women, thrilled with the romance of domesticity.

But outwardly, as I say, the picture was one of almost hysterical confusion. One arrived to dine with Constance in her vast Georgian house near Ascot which was always sprouting so many wings, annexes, and outbuildings that one could never be sure which was the front door. The gardens, frankly, were not beautiful; they made no attempt to be. Their purpose was purely utilitarian, to provide flowers for Constance's business enterprises. True, they contained many rare and surprising treasures, but they had not been designed or planned.

One entered an uncarpeted hall to be greeted with a panorama of flowers and branches and twigs which were so beautiful that one felt breathless. One wandered down long corridors to a room of such sparkling prettiness, all coloured glass and mirrors and bric-a-brac, that one was reminded of a rococo bird-cage. One was seduced by an unexpected cocktail tasting of iced black currants accompanied by an equally unexpected hors d'oeuvres. The evening had begun, and it was sure to be an evening of delight. Finally, one dined in the kitchen, on a scrubbed bare table glowing with arrangements of leaves and fruit, with the aforesaid debutantes hovering around in the guise of waitresses, offering dishes which were not only exquisite but, to most of us, unknown. It was as though Constance had gone to some distant planet and filled her basket with strange fruits and vegetables and essences which are not to be found on this earth.

*　　*　　*

So many and so various were the ways in which Constance brightened our domestic lives that it is difficult to choose any single example to illustrate her versatility. But perhaps the most typical was her rediscovery—for that is what it amounted to—of the old roses. It was Constance who first opened my eyes—and the eyes of many other people—to the diversity of their beauty. Never shall I forget an evening in June when I arrived early for dinner and found myself alone in the bird-cage room, standing in front of one of the prettiest wall-vases I had ever seen, of delicately moulded ormulu with crystal drops. Poised in this vase was a group of old roses of such loveliness, such glowing richness, that the spirit of Boucher might have been tiptoeing round the room, touching up the petals with a spectral brush. In terms of painting the solid background was blocked in with the velvety purple Cardinal de Richelieu, which mingled with the lighter purple William Lobb. The high-lights were provided by a rose that looks as if it were made of striped cherry-coloured satin called Camaieux, and a spectacular beauty, white with flaunting stripes, known as Variegata di Bologna. The effect, as I suggested, was of a group by Boucher; indeed, as one half closed one's eyes, one was tempted to personify the blossoms, to weave stories round them, and to see through the ebb and flow of the silken colours the ghosts of lovely ladies.

*   *   *

I suggested above that Constance, by the creation of her designs, was 'writing a fragrant page of history'. It would perhaps be truer to say that she was rewriting it. Unlike most of her rivals and her imitators she was a highly educated woman; she had steeped herself in the work of the classical flower painters, from the fantasies of van Heem and van Huysman to the baroque masterpieces of Joseph Nigg; and when you saw her carelessly dispose a cluster of roses you realized that Fantin-Latour was no stranger to her. This classical background was also evident in her choice of vases; she never used the modern abominations which are so popular with the average floral decorator; the bloated, bogus urns, the sharp, black vases, the arty plates and platters. She spent almost as much time and trouble with her vases as with the flowers which they were to hold, and often her choice of a container dictated the entire design. Once, when we were prowling round the antique shops of Windsor, she found an old Italian tazza on a dusty shelf, carved from a marble that was almost black, veined with streaks of violet. She picked it up, held it to the light, and asked me: 'What would you put in this?' At random I said: 'Purple grapes.' She nodded. 'Of course. But what else?' I suggested deep red roses, terracotta tobacco flowers and Black Prince dianthus, which is white, flecked with dark violet. She took it home and made a design of precisely these materials, but she had the genius to add a long spray of brilliant scarlet currant tomatoes which were smaller than the grapes themselves.

99

You may see this design, on which she played many charming variations, illustrated in colour in her book *Summer and Autumn Flowers*.

If we had to sum up her quality in a single phrase I would say that she had an 'innocence of eye'. Like all true artists, she saw beauty cleanly and candidly, uncluttered by literary associations or social conventions. Thus, her visits to the kitchen garden were as fruitful as her visits to the herbaceous border; she would return with baskets of blue cabbage leaves, the foliage of young carrots, the leaves of rhubarb spreading like parasols over their bright pink stems, long drooping clusters of red and white currants, as gay and sparkling as costume jewellery. She even found beauty in the rubbish heap, for it was on her own rubbish heap, one autumn morning when she was collecting flowers for a party, that she found a pile of dead hydrangea heads, which had been chopped off by a young gardener who evidently did not know his business. She rescued them and arranged them in a long trough over an old chimney-piece of unpolished pine; with their strange spectral colours of green and rust and ivory they were the sensation of the party and on the following morning they made headlines in one of the gossip columns. Indeed, Constance had cause to regret those dead hydrangeas, for the public came to regard them as a sort of Spry trade-mark, and whenever her rivals wished to denigrate her they would smile sweetly and say: 'Don't you think one can have just a *few* too many dead hydrangeas?'

Let us close this little tribute in a way that I believe Constance would have wished, by returning to the arrangement of old roses which she had made on that unforgettable evening in June; for it was through these flowers, which she did so much to rescue from oblivion, that she would most desire to be remembered.

And since Constance was a strictly practical woman, who would have had little use for a garden book that was all ecstasies, let us make some . . .

PRACTICAL NOTES

The first thing to remember about the old roses—unless you wish to be bitterly disappointed—is that they have a very short flowering period. Generally speaking they don't come out before June and by mid-July they are over. No sign of a second crop, no freak blossoms suddenly gleaming through the frosts of late October. Therefore, if you have a limited space, you must heave a deep sigh, and bow your head, and mutter to yourself that life has been exceptionally beastly to you and go without them.

Another thing to remember is that they are very straggly, like women who leave things littered all over the bedroom. More than any other flower, they put me in mind of certain women, women who have such beautiful faces that they can afford—or think they can afford—to forget their gloves and their stockings and the back of their necks. (No woman should ever forget the back of her neck, but that is a subject which must be reserved for another volume.) Therefore, once again, if you have a limited space, you must heave a deep sigh and bow your head, etc. etc.

Finally, if your space is not so limited (and to me they are so entrancing that I would have at least one specimen, even if I were confined to a back-yard), what sorts should you choose? I would suggest all the varieties named in Constance's bunch. (See above.) To these I would add:

Rosa gallica versicolor. You may know this under the name of *Rosa mundi* or *Fair Rosamund.* Of all the old striped roses, this is the one that keeps its stripes most tidily—pale pink on a background of light crimson. In some of the old roses the stripes become vague and diffused, so that the effect is of a shot fabric. In the *versicolor* they remain as clear as on a Regency silk.

Moreover, this rose, in some gardens, seems to have a magic power of calling back its own ancestors, and producing —while it still keeps its own habit—a side bush of *Rosa gallica officinalis*, from which it is descended. Please remember that rose in any case, whether it comes to you by accident or from the nurseryman. It is lustier than the *Rosa mundi*, a brave, bold rose that might have been worn in battle, and probably was, for legend tells that it is the original Red Rose of Lancaster.

Now for a contrast. The most feminine flower in the world is *Rosa gallica*, Duchesse d'Angoulême. There is nothing brave or bold about this beauty; she is of the palest pink, with petals of striped silk, she blushes in the sunlight, and she is inclined to droop her head. When she does this, you may fear that she is swooning; not at all, it is merely her way. And a very endearing way it is, for if you wish to arrange a bowl of mixed roses, the graceful droop of the Duchesse d'Angoulême enables you to make all sorts of delightful designs.

One of the charms of the old roses is that so much history is written into their petals. They have been gathered from seeds scattered over the tomb of Omar Khayyam; they have nestled on the bosoms of women who have changed the fate of nations. Such a one is Belle de Crècy, which was originally raised in the gardens of Madame de Pompadour at Crècy, and is certainly a tribute to that lady's taste. The colour is, literally, indescribable, because you never know what you are going to get. It opens as a soft pink, but swiftly in the sunshine it becomes suffused with mauves and violets.

Just as their petals are laden with history so they are fragrant with poetry. Of all that have ever been written about roses, the much-quoted lines of Walter de la Mare are perhaps the most evocative.

> Oh! No man knows
> Through what wild centuries
> Roves back the Rose.

And here is a quatrain by Marvell, which has always seemed to me the quintessence of peace. He dreams of a time:

> When only gardens had their towers
> And all the garrisons were flowers;
> When only roses arms might bear
> And men did rosy garlands wear.

Practical notes indeed! If we go on like this we shall end up with an essay on greenfly in blank verse. So let us finish with a bleakly prosaic statement about this pest, by which the old-fashioned roses are especially afflicted. The only effective cure I have ever discovered for this abomination is a product called Tritox, which you water into the roots, at intervals of about a month. (The directions are on the bottle.) It is absorbed by the plant and seeps into the leaves, and as soon as the greenfly alight on the leaves they swoon away. It really does work, it is very cheap, and it eliminates all the boring business of spraying.

I should add that I have no acquaintance with Mr Tritox, nor Mrs Tritox, nor any of the little Tritoxes, if such there be. But I think that after this they really ought to send me a free bottle.

CHAPTER NINE

ROSES AND SHADOWS

CONSTANCE and her friends used sometimes to play
that dangerous little game in which one interprets
one's best friends in terms of birds and beasts, flowers
and food, and even public monuments. What is X's dish?
A raspberry blancmange. What is she as a bird? A moulting
budgerigar. And her flower? A corsage of Parma violets,
left on the dressing-table overnight, and slightly smeared
with lipstick.

Sometimes, as you may imagine, a note of acidity crept
into these analyses. Once, at a party, the victim was Noël
Coward and it was Constance's turn to define him in terms
of architecture. Without a moment's hesitation she replied:

'The Nelson Column entirely wreathed in pale pink hydrangeas.' Which might, or might not, have pleased the Master. On balance, I think that he might have liked it, because it is the sort of thing he could have said himself.

This may seem an odd way to continue our discussion of roses with which we ended the last chapter. But the link is there, though it is tenuous. When it came to my turn, and Constance had to name my own personality flower, she looked suddenly distressed. Not because she was held back by any absurd social restraints—she could have said: 'the blossom of a broad bean covered with blackfly' for all I cared, and she would not have been so far from the mark—but because she was, I think, more than faintly psychic.

At length she said: 'Whatever you are, you are not a rose.'

'Why do you say that?'

'Because. . . ' Her kind little face was pink with embarrassment. 'Because you aren't. And I think that this silly game has gone on long enough.'

*　*　*

For many years I have been writing about flowers, singing their praises in many thousands of words. Though the words may not always have been wise, they always came from the heart.

But until this day I have never been able to bring myself to write about roses. About every other flower that blows, from the first aconites that drop like golden coins from January's frozen fingers, to the last of the little Kaffir lilies that keep their faint flames flickering when the year draws to a close. But I have never been able to write about roses. Nor even to love them, as they should be loved.

Why?

There is a curious psychological reason for this, with which I will not bore the reader, beyond saying that roses are poignantly associated in my mind with the long-drawn-out family tragedy which shadowed the years of my childhood. As a result of this tragedy my whole approach to the rose problem (the word 'problem' is in itself a psychological give-away) is somewhat crazy. Like the woman in that terrifying short story by a neglected American master, Carl Van Vechten. It was called 'The Blue Rose', and it was about a rich old lady who lived in a ruined Southern house—the sort of dream tenement so often and so profitably erected by Tennessee Williams—trying to cultivate a blue rose. There came a day when at last she knew she had succeeded. The rose was in bud; its petals promised a brilliant blueness; there was no time to waste. She must give a party to celebrate its opening. The guests were summoned from far and wide, the candles were lit, the carriages trundled down the weedy drive, the last of the champagne was dragged up from the cellar, and a toast was drunk to the Blue Rose, which was due to open at dawn.

And at dawn the old lady's cries rang up the worm-eaten staircase. 'Come quickly . . . come quickly . . . it has opened!' They tottered down the staircase, rubbing the sleep out of their eyes, and they shambled across the lawn, leaving dewy snake-trails on the grass. They found the old lady standing at the foot of a crumbling wall, her white hair waving in the wind, pointing in ecstasy at the flower which was the crown of her life's endeavour.

'Look at it!' she cried. 'Look at it . . . the blue rose!'

They looked at it. And then they looked away.

For the rose was a brilliant red.

By a curious chance this obsession may perhaps have

added some small value to these pages. Though I have conquered my aversion to some roses, I am still unable to bring myself to grow the roses which flourished in the gardens of my youth. I have concentrated either on the old roses to which Constance introduced me, or on the modern roses which were born long after these unhappy years had passed.

Thus, most of the roses in the small part of my garden which is allotted to them are grey or bluish-silver, not only because these offer the most complete contrast to any of the roses which could recall the past, but because they are in themselves of so rare a beauty. Of all these none is lovelier than Prelude, which more than justified the description you will find in the nurseryman's catalogue. Here it is:

Lavender-mauve with deep shadows in the bud, the open flower takes on the delicate lines of an orchid, for which the soft green of the foliage is a perfect foil.

Perhaps the reason why the grey and silver roses have not yet 'come into their own' is because most people grow them in the wrong way, planting them indiscriminately among the more gaudy varieties. This is the surest way to destroy their beauty, as I found when I planted half a dozen Prelude in front of a group of Sultane. The gold and vermilion flames of Sultane seemed to scorch the delicate blossoms of Prelude, which lost all their subtlety and looked as though they were going into a decline; the colour of the petals recalled the shadows under the eyes of a consumptive. You cannot mix these roses with any that are not of their kind—except, of course, white.

This applies especially when you are arranging them. In a bunch of mixed roses, they are lost, but in a silver bowl, companioned by the snow-white of a rose like Message or set against a few silver leaves of *Senecio cineraria* they compose a ravishing bouquet, which might be held in the white fingers of the princess in Swan Lake.

An exquisite companion to plant near Prelude is Sterling Silver which may be described as Prelude with a silver sheen and a hint of lavender.

To conclude this brief list, let us celebrate that quite extraordinary rose Brownie. I first saw a cluster of Brownies (who chooses these hideous names?) at the Chelsea Show a couple of years ago. They were superbly grown and they were cunningly arranged in a pewter bowl which was a perfect foil to their unique colour—*café au lait*, lit with gold. These strange newcomers were drawing the crowd, but most of the comments were unfavourable; there were a great many tut-tuts and shakings of the head. Whoever *heard* of a brown rose? Who would *want* a brown rose? It was all wrong; it was against Nature, that was what it was. So the crowd gaped and passed by. But I ordered a dozen.

I have never been able to make up my mind whether the Brownies are to be numbered among my failures or my successes, because they have never been quite the same two years running. They seem to be exceptionally sensitive to the weather, not only to the amount of sunlight but to the degree of humidity. In full sun they quickly fade, and in times of drought they sulk; maybe they are pining for the warm mists and shifting shadows of their native Ireland. When these conditions obtain they are—to me—of the greatest beauty, particularly in the aforesaid pewter, on a walnut table.

But even when the weather is fickle they have a habit of giving what one might call 'star performances' which are so thrilling and so unpredictable that one hurries across the lawn every morning before breakfast to find out what they have been up to during the night. Thus, one year they decide to make their debut in brown and suddenly, as though they were doing a quick change in the middle of an act, to switch to a ravishing carmine underpainted with sepia. One cannot avoid the theatrical metaphor—it was like something out of the *Folies Bergère*, where a flick of the light changes the petticoats of the chorus girls.

So I remain faithful, in my fashion, to the Brownies, and I think that you might well indulge in at least a transitory affair with one or two of them.

And there we will say goodbye to the roses. Maybe I should not have written about them at all. The shadow still lingers.

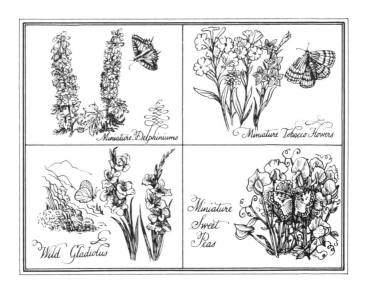

Miniature Delphiniums

Miniature Tobacco Flowers

Wild Gladiolus

Miniature Sweet Peas

CHAPTER TEN

ANTI-BROBDINGNAG

IT has often struck me as strange that whereas the furniture of the modern house grows smaller and smaller, the plants in the modern garden grow larger and larger. Today, a Victorian wardrobe is almost unsaleable; in the average poky bedroom it could not possibly be accommodated. Our rooms have shrunk as our prosperity has swollen. But though our gardens have suffered a similar diminution, the horticulturists seem blandly unaware of the fact. From America comes news of six-foot gladioli, chrysanthemums with heads like footballs, pansies as big as your fist. The advertisement columns in the American gardening magazines have a Hollywood ring; everything is super-colossal and ultra-gigantic. Nor are we far behind in this tendency. At the last Chelsea Show there were delphiniums taller than guardsmen. They had been forced and cosseted and interbred until they no longer looked like delphiniums at all. They were rather frightening, staring out at the crowds with blank blue eyes as big as saucers—flowers from a world of science fiction.

I cannot believe that the average gardener welcomes this trend. It is all very well if you are a dowager duchess of stately stature, with a large retinue of slaves and borders fifteen feet deep. But such ladies, alas, are few and far between; most of us have to do with very little space. So here are a few suggestions for those who must work on a miniature canvas, beginning with the delphiniums.

Miniature Delphiniums. As far as I am aware, there are only three varieties of delphiniums that can be guaranteed to restrain themselves to a height of under fifteen inches. They are:

Tom Thumb. This is rightly described in the few catalogues that list it as 'extra dwarf'. It is a perfect delphinium, but it would be overshadowed by a cluster of bluebells. Best treated as an annual.

Menziesii. Much the same as Tom Thumb, but a deeper blue.

Butterfly. This comes in three colours: blue, lavender, and white. The blue sort has a very pretty brown eye in the middle. In exceptionally good soil they *may* tower up to the giddy height of eighteen inches but never taller. Like Tom Thumb, best treated as an annual. All the beauty of the delphinium family is contained in these modest blossoms. Admittedly they cannot be used as totem poles at harvest festivals, to stun the vicar as he climbs into the pulpit up a staircase of vegetable marrows. But they *are* delphiniums, and if you have cultivated in even the smallest degree the art of 'shrinking', they will delight you for the rest of your life.

Miniature Sweet Peas. In any small garden the sweet pea is something of a problem child. All those sticks! If you have a kitchen garden, of course, the problem does not arise—you merely dig a double trench next to the broad beans and that is that. And all through the summer you have the unalloyed pleasure of sauntering out to gather them, absentmindedly picking a few beans at the same time. (Is there any more subtly delicate flavour than that of a broad bean, taken straight from a pod which is soft and silky as the paw of an exceptionally amiable Siamese cat?)

But for most of us, 'all those sticks' present a problem which is almost insuperable. So what do we do? We invest in miniatures—to be precise 'Sweet Pea Cupid Mixture'. These little plants need no sticks at all. They form a perfectly rounded bush about eight inches high, which is covered with blossoms for a period of at least six weeks. There is only one snag about them, though 'snag' is perhaps too harsh a word. Compared with the ordinary sweet pea they have rather short stalks. And they only come in shades of the colour red. But there are so many reds that it hardly seems to matter— pink and rose and vermilion and flesh and scarlet and cherry. And they *are* sweet peas, and you *can* have them, and they only cost a bob a packet.

Miniature Tobacco Flowers. Whenever I go out into the garden in late November, and look down at the soil from which the tobacco plants have just been uprooted, and see the tens of thousands of tiny seedlings which are already stretching out their small green hands to the dying fires of the wintry sun, I feel puzzled and faintly oppressed by the profligacy of Nature. If it is true that every sparrow falling to the ground is duly registered in a heavenly account book—and I like to hold to this comforting thought—it must equally be true that there is a similar check on every seedling nicotiana, and this is where one's imagination begins to do quite a lot of boggling.

However, let us stick to the good earth. If you invest in the ordinary tobacco flowers, not only will you have unwanted seedlings all over the garden, but you will have a great many problems of untidiness; they are flowers that do not lend themselves to staking, and after a heavy rainstorm they look battered and unsightly. This is where the miniatures come in. There are two dwarfs—White Bedder and *Sanderae*, Crimson Bedder—which never reach a height of over a foot. Both of them keep their eyes open all day, and both form compact cushions of solid blossom. I once found them covering a bank in a Devonshire garden, and the effect was of a sparkling patchwork quilt, with not a speck of earth to be seen.

These are only three examples of popular favourites which can be accommodated in the smallest garden. And whatever the Brobdingnagians may say, I believe that they have a brighter future than any of their gigantic competitors.

* * *

However, of all the flowers which have suffered at the hands of the 'improvers', none has been more monstrously bloated and swollen than the modern gladiolus. Perhaps it is for this reason that it appeals so strongly to the professional flower decorators, who do things to it which should really be forbidden by law. Their favourite trick—especially at public banquets—is to arrange the flowers in open bowls, forcing them into an almost horizontal position so that the blossoms touch the table cloth. Why? Why this passion for perverting Nature, for making flowers lie down when they want to stand up? Once, on a very august occasion in a City Hall, I was so enraged by one of these creations, which was very nearly getting into the turtle soup, that I stealthily pulled out the prostrate flowers from the pinholders and stuck them back again, bolt upright. This had the added advantage of screening, for the rest of the evening, the very unattractive features of the Cabinet Minister who was sitting opposite. But I am afraid that the City fathers thought that it was in very poor taste—as it probably was. One vulgarity begets another.

When you compare the modern *Gladiolus brobdingnagia* with the original wild gladiolus, you realize all that we have lost in the onward march of progress. For here indeed is a little charmer for you! Modest—eighteen inches is the average. A clear, clean purple. A delightful variety of design in the stem, some straight, some curved, some almost pendulous. Asking to be picked, gently and swiftly, and placed in a mixed bunch, for they are most gregarious and very happy in company.

And, of course, brimming with sunlit memories. There must be thousands of British motorists, on their way to the Mediterranean, who have suddenly seen these drifts of purple in the mountains, and stopped the car, and stepped out into the heavy, thyme-laden air, and clambered over the rocks to pick the beckoning gladioli. That is one of the great thrills of travelling, particularly when one is young—to see for the first time flowers growing wild which previously one had only known in cultivation.

Here I must indulge in another moment of autobiography. The first time I ever saw the wild gladiolus, I was, if not exactly dying, as near to it as makes no matter. It was during the war in the remote Indian frontier province of Swat, which runs parallel with a desolate stretch of Afghanistan. My job as a war correspondent had been cut short by a mysterious disease which reached its climax in a little fortress which was temporarily occupied by a rather rag-time section of the Royal Air Force. The amiable young officer in charge gave me to understand that if an operation was necessary there was no anaesthetic available but rum, which would be rather tough on the boys in the mess. Apart from that, he had no official forms to give him any guidance as to the disposal of the corpses of superfluous literary gentlemen. Didn't I think it might be a good idea, old chap, if I got cracking on the old stretcher, and see if I couldn't make it down to the hill-station where, doubtless, something would be 'laid on'?

So a party was organized to carry me away on a stretcher. I do not remember much about it, except the reek of drugs, the hot sun beating down, hour after hour, the dark, sweating faces of the bearers, and an occasional lucid interval in which I looked up to the sky and observed that the vultures were wheeling overhead. As an inveterate reporter, I made a mental note of those vultures. Wings like charcoal against the cloudless blue; black ushers to the gates of heaven; all rather beautiful; linking up with the Parsee religion; must remember to look up Zoroaster, if I ever got out of this; and then . . . darkness again.

But there were two lucid intervals. The first came when I suddenly opened my eyes and saw a field of striped tulips— the same delicate pink and white tulips which danced through the old Dutch flower picture hanging in my study at home. I was sane enough to realize that I had to have some of those tulips, and I lay sweating in the shadow of a flame tree while the bearers dug up a cluster of the bulbs.

Then there was darkness again, until once more I woke up, and saw what seemed to be a flowing robe of purple. It was not the hem of the robe of the Almighty. As the pain increased, my eyes were jerked back into focus and I realized that we were passing through a field of wild gladioli—a magic purple field, with the flowers whispering to themselves in the merciful shadow of a little hill. Somehow or other I sat up, and indicated that I wanted a bunch of gladioli. I got them, and held them tight. There and then I decided that all this nonsense about dying had got to stop, for while there were flowers like this in the world I had to have another garden to plant them in. Where that garden would be and when it would be created, I did not know. But I felt that it would surely come to pass. And it did.

PRACTICAL NOTE

Until the 1962 Chelsea Flower Show I was under the impression that the wild gladiolus—*illyricus*—was unobtainable in this country. However, while wandering round the exhibits, I discovered one firm that lists it, together with several other very ancient garden species, including the rose-pink *communis* and the bright carmine *segetum*. These are among the six wild varieties listed in Robinson's classic *English Flower Garden*. You will find the name of this firm in the appendix.

I seem to have omitted to mention one of the great virtues of this flower; it is almost as hardy as the daffodil. There is no need to lift it in the autumn, though in very cold districts it might welcome the protection of a covering of bracken.

If you are unable to obtain corms through the usual commercial channels, your best course is to buy a motor-car (these vehicles are in plentiful supply), to transport it to the mountains of Northern Spain in the month of April, and to drive round at random, keeping a weather eye open for little splashes of purple among the rocks. After a few weeks you are almost certain to have collected quite a sizeable clump of corms at a cost which could scarcely be regarded as excessive. However, I must issue a word of warning. In order to avoid getting into trouble with the customs you would be well advised to arm yourself in advance with a permit form for the importation of plants and seeds. These admirable documents are provided, in return for a stamped addressed envelope, by the Ministry of Agriculture and Fisheries.

*   *   *

Now for some miniature shrubs and trees.

Every autumn, if you like going for walks in the suburbs, and peering over people's railings, you will see nice little gardens, all set for the scene of future tragedy. A pocket-handkerchief of a lawn, for example, and bang in the middle of it a weeping willow, with a tiny, circular bed round it, filled with seedling wallflowers. It looks so sweet and endearing at the moment, with its slender stem, five feet tall, and its graceful arms caressing the lawn. Who would guess that in ten years' time it will be a lusty, ravening giant of a tree, whose roots will suck the lawn dry while its branches plunge the front parlour into permanent darkness? And what about those two little Lawson cypresses on each side of the front door? For a year or two their owners will be able to talk baby language to them, and pat them on the head as they pass through the front door. But in ten years time, if those cypresses stay where they are, nobody will be able to get in through the front door.

Will people never learn? A hundred to one the answer is no. But in the next few paragraphs there are some hints which *might* avert just a few of these quite unnecessary tragedies.

Let us begin with that ravishing shrub which is so frequently misnamed 'syringa'—the mock orange, whose proper name is philadelphus. People with small gardens nearly always plant the variety called Virginal which grows at a fantastic pace. In a single year its branches may put on an extra six feet. If you want to live your entire life on an exclusive diet of mock orange, by all means plant Virginal. But if you would like rather more variety, shun it like the plague. Plant one of the miniatures, which are just as beautiful, rather more sweetly scented, and far slower in growth. The best varieties are Beauclerk and Belle Etoile. I bought specimens of each of these four years ago and they have remained almost static.

Now for the cherries. If I were artistic dictator of this country I would make it illegal for any householder, during the next twenty years, to plant another specimen of *Prunus* '*Kansan*', popularly known as Hisakura, the gaudy double pink cherry which every spring erupts like an infectious rash down thousands of suburban avenues. This shade of pink should never be planted in isolation, particularly against a background of new red brick. Like some of the pinks in the pictures of Matisse it comes into its own only when it is set against less luscious tints—colours, as it were, with a squeeze of lemon in them, to take away the taste of the sugar. (There are some admirable examples of this sort of planting in Kew, where the '*Kansans*' are mingled with the cool moonlit ivory of the Ukon and the large-flowered white of the Tai Haku. But apart from the sickliness of its colour this cherry has the added drawback of growing, and growing, and growing. As it is a comparatively new introduction, the average gardener does not seem to realize this, and I have heard people who should know better referring to it, and writing about it, as though it never outgrew itself. I could show them specimen 'Hisakuras', planted by innovators a century ago, with trunks the size of full-grown oaks and branches to match.

For these reasons I would substitute:

Prunus Amanogawa. This has one unique advantage for the small garden; it never spreads. Growing as straight as a Lombardy poplar, it keeps itself to itself, not only above the soil but below it, for unlike the poplar family, its roots do not fan out. Moreover, unlike the gaudy 'Hisakura', it is fragrant, and of the most delicate shade of shell pink.

But perhaps you still hanker after a weeping willow? And I fully sympathize with you, because in a small garden, weeping trees—by a curious paradox—are the life and soul of the party. But why must it be a willow, which weeps to such excess? Why not one of the trees whose lachrymosity is less abandoned? At this moment I wish I could take you out to see my small pond, over whose waters two exquisite little weepers are leaning. One is a laburnum (*Laburnum alpinum pendulum*). It is only about seven feet tall, and I shall probably be dead before it grows up another foot. Its arms hang straight down the trunk and each year they are decorated by another set of golden fingers. They reach just low enough for the gold to be reflected in the water, and very lovely this small patch of colour looks when the goldfish flash below it, the red gleam of the fish rippling through the pale glint of the tinted pond. In about ten years, I reckon, the fingers of the tree will be touching the surface of the water and then we shall see what we shall see. Whatever it is, I suspect that it will be beautiful.

On the other side of the pond there is a tree that you will not see in most people's gardens, the willow-leaved pear, by name, *Pyrus salicifolia pendula*. I planted this in order to have a foil of silver to offset the gold of the laburnum. It is one of the most rewarding of all the trees in the garden, pure gleaming silver, starred with white flowers in April. True, it is weeping rather more rapidly than I had bargained for, at the rate of about a foot a year, so that it will not be long before the silver leaves are flecking the water. When they do, I shall simply cut them off. As a compensation, it shows no signs of putting on any top growth at all.

A word of warning. Neither of these trees is in very abundant supply; you can't drop a line to your favourite nurseryman and order a dozen, just like that. But I know of one or two places, some of them off the beaten track, where they can be found. (See appendix.) If stocks at these places are exhausted, you will have to set off on a treasure hunt of your own—a treasure hunt for gold, and silver, and weeping beauty. I can imagine few more pleasing diversions.

A last word about conifers, in the faint hope that I may deter just one eager housewife from planting a Cedar of Lebanon in a bed that is already overcrowded by three aubretias and a plastic stork. If you have space for only one conifer your best bet is one of the junipers, *Juniperus communis hibernica*, whose maximum height is twelve feet. This has a very small 'spread', so that you can use it architecturally to give the effect of columns. Then there are two of the *Chamaecyparis lawsoniana* family, *Fletcheri* and *Pottenii*, both of which have a delicate grape-like bloom of silvery blue;

or the variety *Ellwoodii*.

But here, among the conifers, we reach a stage where you should really put this book down—if you have not done so long ago!—in order to pay a visit to the nurseries. Every conifer has a definite personality of its own and which proclaims itself from its earliest youth, and to buy a tree, even a baby, from a catalogue is as foolish as to adopt a child by parcel post.

A Note on the Use of Tubs and Pots

A miniature world of beauty remains persistently unexplored by the many gardeners who are not 'tub-conscious'. Consider the queen of all flowering shrubs, the rhododendron. There must be tens of thousands of people who go through life without a single rhododendron for two reasons, both of them false. Either they say, 'We cannot have a rhododendron because there is no room for one,' or they say, 'We cannot have a rhododendron because there is lime in our soil.'

But there is always room for a rhododrendon if you will only make use of tubs. In the courtyard of the church of St James's, Piccadilly, there are rhododendrons in quite modest-sized tubs which to my knowledge have been standing there for nearly twenty years. Some of them are over six foot tall, and in the spring they are a mass of blossom. True, their leaves are grimy, they could do with a generous top dressing and they obviously don't get enough water. But these simple attentions, surely, would be given to them if they were in your own garden. Maybe one of the reasons why one so seldom sees tub-grown rhododendrons is because many gardeners imagine that their period of life must necessarily be limited, and that in a couple of years their roots will burst through the bounds of the tubs. This is an illusion. Of course they will not grow as freely as if they were unrestricted, but they are so shallow-rooted and so naturally adapted to accommodating themselves that they flourish, as we have seen, for at least half a life-time. After which, you might feel that they had earned a more commodious home. And though I am the first person to worry about the feelings of plants, and all too prone to anthropomorphism, I cannot believe that these twenty years will have been unhappy for them, nor that they will have had the feeling of being imprisoned.

Eucalyptus

Catanache

Ceratostigma

Morning Glory

Caryopteris

ON HAVING THE BLUES

EVERY author with any large number of books to his credit discovers as the years go by that one of the surest ways of gaining popularity is to ensure that his book contains a reasonable number of errors—a fault in spelling here, a misquotation there. This immediately puts the reviewers in a good humour. 'It is to be regretted,' they write, smacking their lips, 'that Mr X, in his otherwise scholarly work on Balzac, should have omitted to compare the first edition of *Une Ténébreuse Affaire* with the corrected proofs of this work as revealed in the Zweig collection.' Etc. etc. After this lofty reproof they feel at liberty to give the work their patronage. When one is writing a long detective novel a few lapses are quite essential—and, as far as I am concerned, un-avoidable, however carefully the story is checked and re-checked. For surely most readers feel cheated if they do not find at least one flaw in the argument, one piece of false deduction, one herring which is just a shade too red. Other-wise they would not write with such gusto to put one right. 'A most ingenious entertainment,' they are kind enough to say, 'and you had me fooled till the last page. But *what* a pity you made Mr Green take the three-thirty from Paddington, because it does *not* stop at Andover, and even if it did he could not possibly have reached his house in time to receive the anonymous letter, because if it had been posted in Munich on the *fourth* . . . ' Etc. etc.

What has this got to do with gardening in general and with blue pimpernels in particular? Everything. Years and years ago I wrote a book in which I described a Siamese cat whose eyes were as 'blue as a pimpernel', and ever since then people have been taking up their pens to tell me that pimpernels are not blue, but red. Empires may fall, dictators may come and go, but still the letters come. 'Such a charming book,' they say, 'and I am lending it to *all* my friends.' (For your in-formation, this is the one remark that is guaranteed to throw an author into transports of rage.) 'But why that curious lapse on page 187? Why as *blue* as a pimpernel? Surely you must be aware that all pimpernels are scarlet?'

I am aware of nothing of the kind, in spite of Baroness Orczy, who is usually quoted as a witness by most of my correspondents. There certainly *is* a scarlet variety (*Anagallis arvensis*) which hails from the Mediterranean and springs up among the stubble in our native fields in midsummer. But the true perennial pimpernel, *Anagallis linifolia*, is among the most radiant blues in nature, glowing even more brightly than the gentian, with rather the same quality that one sees in old stained glass windows when the morning sun is shining through them. There is a variety called *phillipsii* of especial beauty, which makes a very precious addition to the winter greenhouse if the seed is sown in July. Although this species is perennial in nature, it should be treated as an annual in gardens.

*   *   *

Blue is such a glorious colour in the garden that we can hardly be surprised to find so many attempts to produce it artificially. The search for a blue rose will continue as long as roses bloom, and the rhododendron experts never tire in their efforts to produce blossoms of a purer blue. At the moment they have succeeded with only two varieties that are readily available, Susan and Blue Danube, and even these still retain a faint hint of the common purple *ponticum* from which they are descended.

But of all the flowers that we attempt to 'blue', none is more widely treated than the hydrangea, so much so indeed, that a considerable industry has grown up to meet the demand. The old habit of burying rusty iron round the roots has given way to the simpler method of watering them with a chemical compound, whose basis is alum or aluminium sulphate.

But—and it is a very big but—this technique will be totally ineffective on any but an acid soil, as you will surely learn if you read the directions on the packet. Unfortunately, in gardening matters, a great many people quite obviously do not read the directions on the packet. Year after year they go on blueing away, and year after year they find themselves greeted by the same old shocking pink—or worse, a pink that looks ashamed of itself, like the face of an over-made-up woman suffering from a hangover. Don't they know what an acid soil *is*? For the hundredth time, and solely for the benefit of the newcomers at the back of the class, an acid soil is one that contains the minimum of calcium necessary to support plant life. In soils where this minimum is exceeded, neutralizing chemicals are largely ineffective. And even on what we call a 'lime-free' soil not every variety will produce a perfect blue. The best sort, as I think most experts will agree, is called Vicomte de Vibraye. Oddly enough, this is a vivid shade of rose before treatment, but it turns into a glorious colour without any hint of artificiality. (Incidentally, one pleasant way of changing hydrangeas on a lime-free soil is to buy an aluminium teapot and pour the tea-leaves round them. Apparently some of the aluminium is absorbed in the tea-leaves. This process may take longer, but I fancy that it produces a more pleasing shade of blue.)

One last word about hydrangeas—never cut the heads off. They flower on the last year's shoots and a really nipping frost can put paid to the summer's blossom. Some people may object that the old heads look untidy; maybe they do. But try to forget the untidiness and think of them as nice little tents protecting the flowers to be. If this is too whimsical for you, cover them with bracken, which will almost certainly blow off, and leave the garden looking untidier than ever. Failing this, forget about hydrangeas altogether, and concentrate on spinach.

* * *

I am deliberately neglecting blues which everybody

knows, in order to bring to your notice some of the blues that are less frequently encountered. In an earlier chapter I mentioned two spring flowers that are too rarely grown: the blue cowslip and the blue polyanthus. Let us set the clock forward to high summer, and make a little list to which you might care to refer when you are refurbishing the border.

Quite one of the prettiest blues in the whole garden is the very free-flowering *Catananche caerulea major*, which bears the endearing nickname Cupid's Dart. It grows on stems about two feet tall; in colour it is a Nattier blue and in design it is not unlike a very delicately petalled double daisy. This flower, which could not be easier to grow, must be praised for several qualities apart from its colour. For example, it has a very long flowering period; it comes out in June and then, in September, just when you are beginning to think that like Jane Austen's Mary Bennet it has 'delighted us long enough', it starts all over again and blooms until the first frosts. Moreover, the blooms are semi-perpetual, without the scruffy rather cardboardy texture of some 'everlasting' flowers. The sole disadvantage of this most valuable plant is that it is apt to die back in a hard, damp winter. But it is worth sowing again and again.

Perhaps the common morning glories, those flamboyant trumpets of the convolvulus family that bring into our gardens the skies of the Mediterranean, can hardly be excluded from the category of 'flowers that everybody knows', which I am trying to avoid in this section. But there are morning glories and morning glories, and there are also certain very elementary errors which many people make in growing them. Firstly, they buy inferior seed. For the best variety, which is a comparative newcomer to the market, see the appendix. Secondly, when they sow them in the open air, they put them in too early, deluded by the fickle suns of April. May is quite soon enough, because as soon as they feel the warmth in the soil around them, they race ahead. (They can be sown at the end of March in a frame or cold greenhouse.) But the commonest mistake that most people make is to plant them so that the flowers are in full morning sunlight. If you do this they will certainly look very beautiful before breakfast, but they will have started to droop before the coffee is cold and by noon they will have completely shrivelled up. So plant them where the sun does not reach them till the afternoon. In spite of their name they will still bloom in the morning, but they will also last all day.

What is your least favourite time in the garden? Constance Spry once said that the only month in which she really didn't mind being away was August, and though it sounds rather a strange choice I can understand what she meant. The borders are beginning to look rather tatty and faded, like a touring musical in need of a change of costume. The roses have not yet started their second crop, the chrysanthemums are only just beginning and it is too early for any autumn colour.

But if you love blue there are two shrubs which in August are just coming into brilliant flower, and for this reason alone more people should grow them. Let us swallow their names. (Why, oh why, are we not allowed to garden in plain English?) The first is:

Ceratostigma willmottianum. (Somehow it looks less forbidding if you write it on a single line. Or does it?) This is related to plumbago, the pale blue creeper that used to be the pride of so many Victorian conservatories. But there is nothing pale about this beautiful little shrub, it is deep, deep blue—Botticelli blue—with flowers like tiny stars. It was the particular favourite of an old lady called Miss Mint, whom I once put in a book. She used to keep her Christmas cards throughout the year, neatly stowed away in a handkerchief drawer, where they gradually acquired a faint flavour of dried lavender. They were nearly all of religious subjects, for Miss Mint was not one to speak of her faith in whispers, and her friends respected her convictions. And so there were many oleographs of the Magi under dark blue skies and the Virgin against a heavenly blue background and angels walking across fields of azure. All these blues, every August, Miss Mint took out of her handkerchief drawer, and arranged on her mantlepiece. Having done so she took herself to the garden with a pair of nail scissors and spent a very happy hour snipping off tiny blue stars, which were then carried back to the cottage in one of the aforesaid handkerchiefs. After which the stars were floated in all manner of miniature receptacles—eggcups, salt-cellars and the like—and reverently set in front of the religious back-cloth, where they seemed to twinkle. On one hot Saturday afternoon I said to Miss Mint that the whole thing put me in mind of a little altar. To which she agreed though, I fancy, with some reservations, for she was what is known as 'Low Church'.

The other late blue, flowering in August alongside the plumbago, is called *Caryopteris 'Ferndown'*. They 'deal' perfectly together—as they used to say about congenial couples in the days of the Regency—for this is a pale powdery blue, a Boucher to set against the Botticelli. I first encountered a wild form of this plant on a remote beach in Corfu, growing in great abundance close to the water, with its roots in almost pure sand. This gives a clue to the sort of conditions which it obviously prefers; it has the same tastes as a tamarisk.

In Corfu it formed a dense bush of six feet, which was very

convenient, because it formed an admirable hiding place from the attentions of a guide called Sophocles who, if not the biggest bore in Europe, was assuredly the biggest bore in Corfu.

Sophocles, who was short, hirsute, and heavily moustached, had a consuming desire—to acquire a lady's wig; whether to enact a role in the local dramatic society or for some less innocuous purpose, I was never able to discover. For some extraordinary reason he imagined that I would be able to provide him with this object; it seemed strange to him that any English author, particularly the type of English author who succumbs to the charms of Corfu, should travel abroad without equipping himself with such a necessity. When I told him that I had no wigs, male or female, he looked very pained. Then his face brightened.

'But you will be returning to our beautiful island?'

'I hope so.'

'Then you will buy the wig in London and bring it on your next visit.'

'I shall do no such thing.'

'But Mr Nikos . . . '

'You can buy it yourself on your next visit to Athens.'

'But Mr Nikos . . . if I do that, I must show it to the officer of the customs, and he is my brother-in-law.'

'I can't help that.'

'What will my brother-in-law think when he finds a lady's wig in my valise?'

'I have no idea.'

'It would be impossible.'

'Yes it would.'

'But for *you* it will be easy. So you will buy the wig in London. And I will pay you in drachmas.'

'No.'

A deep sigh. Another sudden face-brightening. 'I will speak to my brother-in-law on your account. I will tell him you do not wish the wig examined. You will give a little present to my brother-in-law. And I will pay you in drachmas.'

'No, Sophocles, *no!* '

Which, in my youth, would have been called 'cue for song'.

So whenever I take pleasure in the misty beauty of caryopteris, I find myself automatically murmuring 'No, Sophocles, no.'

PRACTICAL NOTE

The *Caryopteris 'Ferndown'* is not fussy so long as you remember to treat it like a tamarisk—full sun, good drainage, soil not too heavy round the roots. A sack of sand helps. In England it may be cut down to the ground in a severe winter, but more often only the ends of the branches are affected; you can snip off these dead bits when the green shoots begin to show

Galtonia

Cerastium tomentosun

Senecio ceneraria

Stachys lanata

Hosta

CHAPTER TWELVE

AND THE WHITES

IN the climate of Britain, and in some of the climates of Northern America, it might seem almost eccentric to demand cold white flowers and leaves in summer. We so seldom need them. And yet, every August, in the glossy home-making magazines, we are treated to articles on 'How to Keep Cool in the Garden'. These articles are illustrated by models in the semi-nude, reclining under striped umbrellas, sipping chilled drinks through a straw. As one reads them, in a howling gale, one sincerely hopes that the poor things will not develop double pneumonia.

However, perhaps that is libelling our poor old climate.

We do have—every three years or so—a glorious summer, and even in the worst of seasons there are spells when we would welcome a cooling breeze. It is then that the cold white flowers and leaves come into their own. And even when the heat has passed, they are in themselves so beautiful, and provide so subtle and extensive a range of pale colours for flower decoration, that it does not seem to matter.

Of all these summer snows I would choose, to head the list, the galtonia, of which I made a brief mention in the introduction. You will remember that this was one of those flowers which throughout my gardening career had persistently evaded me. Why, heaven only knows, for though it is not widely grown, and though comparatively few nurserymen list it in their catalogues, there is nothing in the least mysterious about it. And yet, for thirty years I was never introduced to it.

My belated discovery of galtonia occurred in so curious and diverting a fashion that it makes a little story on its own.

I have a charming elderly neighbour whom we will call Lady D. Her passion for flowers is so intense and her reaction so immediate that her friends live in fear that one day she will see a lily on the other side of the road, forget all about the traffic, and run across to greet it, with fatal consequences. Lady D is often my companion on excursions to the various lovely gardens that are open to the public in our part of the world. And here I must confess that her adoration of flowers occasionally leads her to behave in a manner which might not be approved by the authorities. I can best describe this behaviour by explaining that only too often, when we return home, she triumphantly produces from her bag some blossom which she has purloined when nobody was looking—the bell of a rare fuschia which she filched from the cool house at

. . . never mind where, or a large white camellia which was flowering in the corner of the gardens at X.

When one remonstrates with her about this regrettable tendency she looks at one with an expression of the greatest innocence and protests: 'But my dear, it had *dropped!* ' It had, of course, done nothing of the sort. But one does not care to argue with an old lady, so one can only hope for the best, and make a note to keep her under sharper observation on the next excursion.

Well, three summers ago, we went off to visit the gardens at X, which are always almost deserted on weekdays. It was a glorious afternoon, and though it was 'between seasons' there was still a host of giant lilies lighting up the shadows under the oaks. These lilies engaged the attention of Lady D, and she lingered over them for so long that I wandered off to examine something else. When I returned I gave her a searching look. She had left her bag in the car, and she could not possibly have concealed one of those enormous lilies on her person. All seemed to be well until we got home.

And then, she opened her glove and held out her hand.

'What have you been up to this time?'

'It's for you.'

'But what is it?'

'It dropped.'

I made no comment on this outrageous assertion. The stem was still green and had obviously been torn off in a hurry.

'But what *is* it?'

'It's a pod from one of those beautiful white lilies. I thought you might like to plant some of the seeds. When they come up you can give me some.'

'You really must not do these things. One of these days . . . '

She made an impatient gesture. 'I know exactly what you're going to say. One of these days I shall be arrested and sent to prison. Well, if the Tory Government . . . ' (Lady D claims to have communist inclinations) 'can't find anything better to do than persecute poor old ladies for picking up flower pods that have dropped. . . . '

She caught my eye.

'Or *almost* dropped.'

So the argument ended, as always, in laughter.

And I planted the seeds.

They came up as onions.

At least, that was what we thought they were, when the thin spikes appeared in the following spring.

I said to Page, as we bent over them: 'But where on earth did Lady D find onions in the X gardens? And having found them, why should she want to pick them?'

'Beats me. It certainly *looks* like one of onion family.'

'She said she picked it from a lily.'

'Lady D's idea of lilies are a bit vague. Maybe she picked it for a joke?'

'Lady D would never joke about flowers.'

'That's true enough. Anyway, it'll be interesting to see what comes up, when the time comes.'

The time came in August of the following year. We had planted the seedlings in semi-shade, and as the months sped by they grew apace, looking more like onions every day. I was in two minds as to whether they should be pulled up, particularly when the first flower spike appeared, for it was almost indistinguishable from a giant garlic. However, little by little the buds—there were eighteen of them—began to swell, to hang their heads, and to take the shape of bells, until one glorious morning I went out to find that the first of them had fully opened. And it was indeed a snow white bell, like a giant *Leucojum*, six-petalled, with stamens of the palest green. A fortnight later the whole stem was laden with bells which lasted, still glistening, for over six weeks.

When I gathered one of the later flowers, and took it over to Lady D she was like a child to whom one has given some wonderful present. She set it in a slender vase of silver and stared at it in silence. Then she turned to me and said: 'And to think that it had dropped, and that I picked it up!'

PRACTICAL NOTE

The galtonia, as we have observed, is not listed in many catalogues. However, in the appendix you will find the name of a nurseryman who, at the time of writing, can supply bulbs for 6s. a dozen; also the name of a famous nursery who supply packets of seed for a shilling. The mention of seeds reminds me that this is yet another occasion where I am in conflict with the experts. In Robinson's classic *English Flower Garden* it is stated:

> The *Galtonia candicans* (Summer Hyacinth), a noble bulb from the Cape, is increased by offsets from the bulb, or from seeds, *which flower about the fourth year*.

Well, as we have seen, my bulbs flowered in under two.

*　　*　　*

If you study Constance Spry's classic, *Summer and Autumn Flowers*, in which many of her masterpieces are reproduced— and I do not think that 'masterpiece' is too strong a word— you will be struck by the delicate artistry with which she uses white, and the many pale shades that so happily accompany it. Thus, with her madonna lilies which most of us would be well advised to leave severely alone, she had the genius to mingle sweeping branches of the lime tree, stripped of its leaves. The pale lemon of the blossom was an enchanting echo of the golden lily stamens. Again, her keen and innocent eye recognized the neglected beauty of the Portuguese laurel, which the average man would scarcely regard as a flowering shrub at all, associating it with the clipped and distorted monstrosities that one meets in public gardens. But Constance knew how to 'produce' it, arranging it in bold masses on stone chimney-pieces, so that the white flowers appeared like a cascade tumbling over the dark glistening background of the leaves.

And on a white tablecloth, in a white bowl, she disposed thick clusters of white peonies and pale yellow water-lilies, which were as luscious as bowls of Devonshire Cream.

Momentary Diversion: This note should perhaps come in the next chapter, but we will put it here in case we forget. It concerns the use of water-lilies in the house. If you pick a water-lily in full flower and bring it indoors to float in a bowl, it will look ravishing for a few hours; but then it starts to sulk and close up, and next morning it is giving a very good impersonation of an ill-tempered Jerusalem artichoke. The way to prevent this is to take a lighted candle and drop hot wax into the centre of the blossom while the petals are still fully open. This sounds cruel and slightly vulgar but the flowers seem to welcome the treatment. This is a most soothing and satisfactory occupation for a hot Saturday afternoon; all the golds and whites seem to blend together—the gold of the flickering candle, the white of the wax falling on to the golden stamens. As a gesture in favour of world peace, dropping wax on to water-lilies would seem likely to be far more effective than sitting down in the middle of Trafalgar Square.

As we were saying, Constance's use of the whites and the off-whites was inspired—white roses and trails of creamy honeysuckle in an ormulu vase; white roses and pale apricot foxgloves in a golden urn; great sprays of white delphiniums against an ivory screen; white tulips springing from a cluster of silver eucalyptus.

But things are moving so quickly in the gardening world that there are some whites—and even more, some silvers—that Constance did not know, and of all these the most spectacular is afforded by the leaves of a little plant called *Senecio cineraria*, variety Ramparts, which made its debut during the year of her death. I often wonder what she would have made of it in a decoration. I feel that it would have been something sparkling and brittle and exquisitely artificial, like the most rococo form of Venetian glass.

Here is a challenging statement. Apart from the underside of certain tropical ferns, which are so thickly painted with silver that in the dark they have a quality of phosphorescence, by far the most brilliant silver in Nature is afforded by this small treasure. If you dropped a scarf of silver lamé on the lawn, on a cold night, and came out in the morning to find it shimmering with frost, you would reproduce the effect very prettily. When you set it side by side with one of the more common silver-leaved senecios, such as the species *leucostachys*, it shines with an almost arrogant brilliance and the poor *leucostachys* looks as drab as the little girls in the advertisements whose mothers have not used the right washing powder. 'Ramparts' does shine 'brightest of all'. Since it hails from quite a modest nursery it may not be in very large supply. But even if you cannot get it this year, it is well worth waiting for. (See appendix for address.)

*   *   *

White calls to white, as we have suggested before, one white echoing and enhancing another, which is one reason why white flowers are so beautiful against a white wall. For white is not the absence of colour, it is colour in infinite variety, so that an all-white garden is as exciting as the most brilliant border. Of all the pictures I would paint, if I were a millionaire, this would be the first.

The most beautiful all-white garden I ever saw was at Broadlands, in the days before the Mountbattens had it, when it was still the home of Lady Mount Temple. It was, and still is, the dream of a house, with wide lawns sloping down to a river which was curved like the neck of a swan. The white garden lay at about a quarter of a mile from the house, enclosed on all sides by walls of old red brick, and when one entered through the little gate one might have exclaimed that it was 'a veritable fairyland', if one were in the habit of using such expressions. It was laid out inform-ally, with one very wide irregular border, which looked like a snow-drift in high summer—white delphiniums, drifts of white campanulas, white phlox, white Shirley poppies, phalanxes of white Madonna lilies rising from pools of white dianthus. The walls were a riot of that lovely rose, Madame Alfred Carrière, side by side with a magnificent old mag-nolia, whose white blossoms shone like lamps in the green leaves. On the furthest wall she had disposed a flight of white pigeons, which remained strangely still as though in a trance, which was hardly surprising as they were made of china.

Molly Mount Temple was one of the few women whose taste might perhaps be matched with Constance Spry's; there was, indeed, a certain rivalry between the two ladies which, in Molly's case, grew into a positive animosity. She was a strange, tortured creature who was never reconciled to the fading of her beauty. And though she was at heart a kindly person, she developed late in life a sort of waspishness —particularly towards servants—which made staying at Broadlands something of an ordeal.

I shall never forget a June evening when we went for a walk in the kitchen garden, which was immense and furnished with enough asparagus to feed battalions of orphans for months. Everything was immaculate; not a weed on the smooth surface of the cinder paths, not a trace of blight on the heavily laden broad beans. Suddenly Molly stopped in her tracks. There at her feet lay a small trowel which must have been left by one of the gardener's boys.

'Do you see,' said Molly in a strangled voice, 'what I see?'

I did indeed, and I bent down to pick it up.

'No!' she exclaimed. 'Do not touch it. Leave it alone!'

She might have been talking of a high explosive. But she was not looking at me, she was staring to the end of the path, down which Hawkins, the head gardener, was slowly approaching.

He came up to us and touched his cap.

'Good evening Hawkins.'

'Good evening m'lady.'

'This, Hawkins, is Mr Beverley Nichols.'

'Good evening, sir.'

'Mr Nichols is a very famous gardener.'

Hawkins made no comment on this assertion.

She pointed to the trowel. 'Is *this* the sort of thing we like Mr Nichols to see at Broadlands, Hawkins? Garden tools scattered all over the place?'

He bent down slowly and picked it up. When he straightened himself he was very red in the face. Again he touched his cap. 'Good evening, m'lady.'

Molly had given her little wasp sting, and as with the wasp, she had parted with something of herself in doing so. She was tired and dispirited when we walked back to the house, not with Hawkins but with herself. For she was, I repeat, a kindly woman at heart, and when she died she did something which must have made Hawkins forgive her for all her tiresomeness—she remembered him in her will.

How strange are the ways of some very rich people with their gardeners! How seldom they allow themselves to be guided! They obey their doctors' orders, they follow the advice of their lawyers, they do as their stockbrokers tell them, but in the garden they behave like ignorant and arrogant dictators. As a result, a relationship which should be a happy partnership is often soured and embittered.

However, we were supposed to be talking about white.

*   *   *

We made the 'challenging statement' above that the Ramparts variety of the *Senecio cineraria* is the most brilliant silver in nature. But we should not forget its humbler companions in the same colour range. If you have a stretch of grey paving stone, few plants look prettier than the endearing Lamb's Ears (*Stachys lanata*), with its soft woolly leaves that children love rubbing against their noses. In spite of their soft texture they are incredibly tough and can be subjected to the most brutal treatment without coming to any harm. And if there is a wall round your paving stone, the Lamb's Ear will be delighted by the refreshing sight of one of the most tenacious of wall-growers—the old-fashioned Snow in Summer (*Cerastium tomentosum*), with its silver leaves, and its dazzling cushion of white flowers. You can buy seeds of this, but mine just drifted on to the wall, borne by the breeze or dropped by an obliging bird, and there it has stayed ever since.

And what about white leaves? In the garden at Merry Hall this question was easily answered, for I had been lucky enough to inherit several silver maples, which were planted in semi-shade, so that the lower branches produced abundant sprays of leaves that were as white as wax. These leaves were an annual cause of rage and frustration to Our Rose, who longed to use them in her monstrous devices. However, I never let her have any because I am quite certain that she would have plunged the stems into purple ink.

But if you have no silver maples you can have an abundant supply of white and green leaves with the hostas—the plants which our parents knew by the name of 'funkia'. There are two species called *albo-marginata* and *undulata*, whose names explain themselves even if your Latin is rusty, for they are boldly streaked with white, like Connemara marble and curiously convoluted. The degree of white varies, sometimes the whole leaf will be white with only a faint green margin, at other times it will be green with a white stripe, but even then it is gay and elegant, like a Regency silk.

People often ask me what to grow in city gardens, particularly gardens surrounded by high walls, where the sunlight seldom ventures. The hostas probably give us the best answer. Their flowers are on the dim side, like rather dispirited bluebells, but the leaves more than make up for the deficiency.

And here is a small discovery about those leaves—at least, I call it a 'discovery' because I have never seen it mentioned elsewhere. Being almost excessively attached to hostas we grow them in half a dozen varieties, including the sort that used to be called *glauca*, now rechristened *sieboldiana*, whose green leaves, as handsome as those of an aspidistra, have a faint bloom of lavender. Well, one summer, I arranged them in a big white basket in the fireplace, and used them with various white flowers, changing the flowers as they faded but keeping the background of leaves intact. After a while this became rather a bore, so I carried the basket out to the tool-shed, leaves and all, left it in a dark corner, and forgot all about it.

Several weeks passed.

One morning, looking out of the window I noticed that the bracken on the common had begun to turn, which was exciting, for two reasons. Firstly, because bracken is a lovely thing to mix with autumn flowers, such as the common scruffy kitchen garden chrysanthemums, which are the only sort of chrysanthemums that I really like. Secondly, because picking even the smallest snippet of bracken on Ham Common is strictly against the law, which is about the most monstrous thing I ever heard of. Here we are, paying gigantic sums every week to support the Welfare State, working our fingers to the bone in order to provide nougat-stuffed infants with luxury limousines to take them to school . . . and it is against the law to pick even a buttonhole of bracken, with which the entire common is rampant. It does not appear to matter if the aforesaid over-stuffed infants, as they gorge their way down the paths, leave behind them a trail of sticky silver paper, which I have to pick up. Nor if quantities of young couples plunge into the bracken as though they were hurtling themselves into a double-bed and to carry on accordingly. But gather a single frond of the stuff and you've had it. Which is why, every year, I go out in a frenzy of moral indignation, waving secateurs in defiance of all and sundry, and pick a gigantic bunch and carry it home, walking in the middle of the road in the hope of bringing matters to a head.

So I hurried down to the tool-shed to fetch the white basket in which the bracken would be arranged. And then I forgot all about the bracken, for in their dark corner the leaves of the hostas were glowing as yellow as daffodils. The water in which they had been standing had long since evaporated, but they had not withered nor turned brittle nor lost their shape. They had merely turned this glorious yellow, so that they looked as if they had been carved from metal.

Perhaps you may agree that this really does deserve to be classed as a minor 'discovery' in the art of flower decoration. Particularly since the leaves, as I was to discover, lasted till nearly Christmas.

We have strayed a long way from the shades of white we were supposed to be discussing. In the next chapter we will try to be more consistent.

CHAPTER THIRTEEN

WATER MAGIC

I N the first chapter of this book we laid down the following
arbitrary principle: 'A garden without water is not a
garden at all. Even a back-yard should have a miniature
water-lily in a tub.'

Evidently the vast majority of gardeners do not share this
opinion. There are many beautiful gardens in my part of the
world and not one of them has even a sunken bucket in the
rockery. They have sweeping lawns, rich conservatories, and
impeccable borders, but were a thirsty sparrow to land on
their estates it would have to put its head through the scul-
lery window if it needed a drink.

This I find inexplicable. Why—to ask the most obvious
question about this mystery—do all these people quite

deliberately deny themselves the delights of a great and glowing family of water flowers? Though it would not be true to say that we can grow as many flowers in the water, or at the water's edge, as on dry land, it is most assuredly true that even if all our gardens were flooded and turned into lakes, we could still have a most exciting time.

What is the meaning of it? Are the anti-water brigade suffering from some curious complex, some sort of horticultural hydrophobia? Do they fear that they may be fatally bitten by a goldfish, or stung to death by a plague of mosquitos?

Or is it simply a matter of ignorance? Have they never dipped their fingers into a pool on a summer evening, and drawn towards them a spray of the white water-hawthorn which carries in its pretty petals the scent of a country hedge in May? Have they never marvelled at the careless grace of the water crowfoot whose little golden cups are held aloft above the surface, as though a strange procession of water folk were passing underneath? Have they never stared, and gone on staring, at the green, misty tendrils of the water moss, whose fingers are jewelled with a thousand bubbles? Nor studied the infinite variety of colour patterns which are painted on the palette of the pond by the brush of the wind as it ripples the water, playing delicate tricks with golden and purple echoes of the irises at the water's edge?

Above all, are they blind to the beauty of the lilies? The colour range of the water-lily is even more extensive than that of the rose, starting from ice-white, drifting down through all the yellows and golds, taking a sudden plunge into the blues (the blue lilies are all too little grown), and finishing in a flurry of pinks, vermilions and carmines. Moreover, the leaves of the lilies are as lovely as the flowers, not only because of the delicate patterns in which they dispose themselves but because, when the days are shortening and the water is beginning to chill, some of these leaves provide us with a richness of autumn colour with which few trees of the forest can compete. Of all the colour in my garden, towards the end of October, nothing is so vivid as the amber leaves of a miniature lily called *Nymphaea Laydekeri*, enamelled on the dark surface as though they had been painted by a Chinese master on a lacquered screen.

If you think that water is of no importance, answer me this question: how is it that whenever the garden is open to the public the crowds drift automatically to the pond, and stay there till sometimes they have to be asked to move away? Why does *every* visitor do this? If it were only the children, one could understand, because they are obviously interested in the fish. But why do old ladies sit by the side of it dreaming, and young girls stand there as though they were in a trance? Why do I do it myself, on all my little 'tours' throughout the year? Why is it inevitably my first port of call?

We have asked so many questions in this section that perhaps we had better pause, for a moment, and try to answer some of them.

*   *   *

The answer to this strange magnetism of the pond is in some degree a mystic one.

I am rather nervous about reverting to the theme of mysticism in the garden, which has already engaged us in our discussion of the qualities and potencies of the soil, for you may soon begin to suspect that I spend my days wandering about in a white sheet, leaving trails of ectoplasm on the lawn. But how can one avoid it? A pond has all the simple magic of a mirror, and if you can show me a mirror that is *not* magic, I shall be greatly surprised. All mirrors, surely, are magic mirrors by their very nature, but a mirror in a garden, as a small boy once said to me, after reading 'Alice', is 'magicker'. For the mirror on the lawn, the pond, has a life of its own, apart from the life it reflects; not only does it take the clouds and the flowers to itself, but it plays with them, repaints them, and tirelessly repatterns them. As for the other sort of life, the multitude of strange creatures which it conjures up apparently from nowhere, is there not also magic in *them*? How do they get there? One digs a hole in the ground and fills it with water from the tap, and suddenly hey presto, one finds a regatta of water-boatmen shooting across the surface with the greatest skill. Where did they come from— the clouds? But if they were in the clouds why are we not showered with water-boatmen when it rains? And the tadpoles and the frogs—where have *they* come from? Where have they been hiding? In the leaves? In the earth? In the toolshed? Doubtless there is a simple answer to such questions, and in these days of space travel they must seem very naive to a scientific mind, but to me they have a compelling fascination. I never tire of sitting by the edge watching the antics of the minnows, the water-snails, the newts, and all sorts of tiny creatures to which I cannot put a name—uninvited guests, but none the less welcome.

If I have not made my point about the magic of the pond after all these words I shall never make it at all, so let us get down to earth, or rather to water, and try to be practical. We ought to begin by a few words on feeding the goldfish, but before we do that, I would like to 'get something off my chest'. It concerns the use of Polythene.

POLYTHENE PONDS

Every year, when the summer comes round, the gardening magazines are fairly certain to publish idyllic photographs of suburban families gathered on their lawns, gazing in ecstasy at a stretch of water which—so we are given to understand—is contained solely by a lining of Polythene which Dad has gaily tossed into a hole after a few hours carefree digging on a Saturday afternoon. These photographs are really quite touching. Dad reclines luxuriously in his deck-chair, contemplating the result of his handiwork, Mum dabbles her fingers in the water, junior, with a happy smile, launches his sailing boat on to the gentle ripples. Sometimes, to make the picture even more alluring, a young lady of ample proportions stands on the edge, attired in a swimming suit, with her arms lifted above her head as though she were about to dive in. Which, when one comes to think of it, would be ill-advised, as she would assuredly stun herself to death.

Do not believe these pictures. In a mad moment, I once made a Polythene pond. And the reason why I developed a fierce hatred for it before it was even finished can be summed up in two words—damp underwear. That is what it made me think of, from the very first moment when the Polythene was stretched across the hole. This was not a pool. It was old gentlemen's drawers. This had nothing to do with Nature, cupping the rain in her hand. It was unmentionables. Even though the Polythene was black, and practically undetectable, and even though the edges were cunningly concealed with turves, this impelling suggestion of damp underwear remained; I had only to stand by it for a half a minute to feel a chill in my own pants.

You may call this a complex, and maybe it was. But apart

from the psychological complications, the pond very soon began to reveal a number of weaknesses which were never suggested in the advertisements. At the deep end the Polythene began to sag, accentuating the underwear illusion, as though some awful old gentleman's drawers were slowly dropping down. At the shallow end some of it slipped away from the turves, so that streaks of it fluttered in the wind. This drew the interested attention of that king of cats, Oscar, who pounced on it with his beautiful gleaming claws, puncturing it in several places, so that it developed a leak. As if this were not enough, a loathsome scum appeared in some of the pockets, which attracted the goldfish, with fatal results. Twenty-four hours after I had emptied them into this witch's brew—admittedly with many misgivings—they were lying flat on their backs on the top of the water, gasping with distended gills. At the risk of sounding morbidly sensitive, I must confess that the collection of half-dead goldfish in a bucket is not among my favourite occupations.

So much for Polythene ponds. To me, they are an abomination and a desolation. Let us return to the goldfish, and consider them in a less unnatural environment.

FEEDING THE GOLDFISH

It is difficult to be 'practical' about feeding goldfish; they consistently break all the rules. At Merry Hall I had the same sort of pond, the same sort of water-plants, and the same sort of goldfish—bought at Woolworth's—as in my present domain. In the former pond they devoured quantities of fish food and when we gave them fresh ants' eggs—which were only too abundantly available from the ants' nests in the orchard—they leapt out of the water with excitement. Moreover, they became very friendly, answering the tap of a spoon as though it were a dinner-gong, and literally eating out of one's hand.

Nothing like this has happened in the present pond. Precisely the same conditions have produced precisely opposite results. The fish cater entirely for themselves, living, flourishing and multiplying solely on the nourishment provided by the pond itself. When they are offered fish food, they scorn it and peck contemptuously at an air bubble. I deluge them with ants' eggs and they shrug their shoulders. The tap of the spoon sends them briskly for shelter under the leaves of the lilies. They are very grand and golden and glistening, but they could not be less matey and I cannot work up any very tender feelings about them.

Here ends the Nichols lesson on How to Feed the Goldfish. You will find it flatly contradicted by all the experts, but that cannot be helped. I write only of what I know.

However, the experts are certainly right on one point: whether the goldfish eat your fish food or whether they spurn it, whether they like you or whether they ignore you, they will die if you do not provide them with oxygenating plants— one of Nature's most fascinating families, often, like the water-boatmen, appearing from nowhere at all, surviving on practically nothing, living a strange twilit existence in the depths.

You will find a short list of these plants in the appendix.

One last word about the goldfish. How are we going to protect them from the onslaughts of the herons, the king-fishers, and other predatory fowls of the air? In a single morning a couple of hungry herons can clear a whole pond. They usually come in the very early hours of the morning, with a flutter of grey wings over the grey sky, guided by some uncanny instinct that tells them you have provided them with a meal. Sometimes you may be awake, and can shoo them away, but more often you do not discover the tragedy till later. There is always a dark oily streak on the surface to warn you of what has been happening.

Can we prevent this? Here again we come into conflict with the experts. I once asked this same question in the columns of a Sunday newspaper with a very large circulation. There were several hundred replies, setting forth 'infallible' methods of saving fish from birds. Most of these methods were variations on five themes:

1. Stretching a network of wires under the water, in the hope that the birds will catch their feet in it and take fright.
2. Building a small foundation of bricks in the middle of the pond and placing a square of mirror on top so that the water just laps over. Again, the hope is that the birds will take fright.
3. Covering the entire pond with wire netting.
4. Surrounding the pond with brightly-painted wine bottles stuck on the end of bamboos.
5. Glitterers.

I tried 1. and 2. with absolutely no effect; indeed, one early morning I woke up to see a crane standing in the water with its head on one side, gazing at itself in the mirror with obvious satisfaction. As for 3.—covering the whole pond with wire netting—apart from the fact that this would put paid to the lilies, the whole thing would look so hideous that it would be better to have no pond at all. The same objection applies to 4.—the painted wine bottles. This is a device introduced by imported Italian gardeners, and though it may be useful for protecting a row of raspberry bushes it has no place near an ornamental pond.

Worst of all is 5.—the glitterers. One of the subtlest delights of a water garden is the delight of sound; all the miniature music that it makes on a lazy afternoon; the sudden 'plop' as a goldfish rises to catch a gnat, the high sharps and trebles of a tiny fountain, the faint buzz of a dragon-fly, the sigh of the wind in the reeds by the edge. This would be utterly ruined by the snap and crackle of a lot of glitterers.

Then is there nothing that we can do about it? I think there is. After dismissing all the suggestions of the experts we did a lot of hard thinking for ourselves, and one day an extremely efficient lady who had been an air raid warden during the war suggested that what we really needed was a form of air raid shelter. So why not simply lay a few drainpipes on the concrete bottom? They would soon get covered with water-moss and in the summer one wouldn't see them at all. If the fish could only learn to dart into them when danger approached, in the same way that Londoners learned to run for shelter to the tubes, all might yet be well.

This is precisely what we did. And so far, touch wood, all *is* well. The drainpipes have done the trick; indeed, they have been so efficient that soon the pond will be overstocked.

*   *   *

Water-lilies are so simple to grow that there is no need to go into a long technical dissertation about them; it would only put you off. All you have to do is to tie the roots into a small wicker basket filled with loam and a little old cow manure, drop them into the water, and that is that. Naturally they do best in full sun and quiet water, and it goes without saying that you must give consideration to the depth in which you plant them. It would be foolish, for example, to put any of the 'pygmy' varieties into deep water; they would merely drown. However, all such details are concisely set forth in the catalogues of the aquatic nurserymen which you will find in the appendix.

A word about plants for the edge of your pond. I grow mine in three small circular pockets round the edge, made of old bricks. We did not concrete the bricks; we merely arranged them on top of one another as though we were building a castle in the nursery. Then we put in sods of earth, stuck in the roots and that was all there was to it.

Here—keeping to the principle of writing only of what we know, and of what can be 'inspected'—are the three plants in question.

Firstly, the giant kingcup which you see by the side of country streams. This is the earliest flower of the year to offer its face to the pond's reflection, and a very beautiful face it is, brilliant gold, like a big double buttercup. It starts to show a faint gleam just when the crocuses are fading, like a chink of light from a dark room, as the door of winter slowly opens on to spring.

It has the intimidating name of *Caltha palustris plena*, does

Iris kaempferi   *Nymphaea albatross*

best just *out* of water, increases rapidly, and costs 3s. 6d.

Next, the 'clematis' iris, *Iris kaempferi*, which, like Elsa Maxwell's 'ninety-nine most intimate friends', is one of my ninety-nine most beautiful flowers. Indeed, I think it would probably gain a place in the first three—the winner being the Green Dragon lily and the second place being kept open for an endlessly diverting floral argument, never to be finally resolved. No ecstasies about this flower, they would stretch to pages. My favourite is a variety called Dresden China, which is lavender flecked with silver, arising from leaves of very delicately sculptured jade. Four bob.

Lastly, the water plantain, *Pontederia cordata*, commonly known as pickerel weed. This is very 'showy' plant, and why not? An English garden can do with a little flourish, now and then. Not that there is anything coarse about this rampaging creature, merely that it grows with a jungle vigour and throws up its spikes of blue flowers like a firework display in late summer and early autumn, when sometimes the skies are already beginning to frown. The leaves, too, are very beautiful, straight and sturdy and shaped like broad arrows.

There is only one thing to be said against it; if you have a pond as modest as mine you have to be constantly controlling it and keeping it back. In August all sorts of eager white tendrils start creeping through the cracks in the bricks, fingering their way into the mysterious watery world outside, obviously longing to start new colonies. When this happens —unless you want the entire pond to be filled with it, to say nothing of Ham Common, and eventually the greater part of Surrey—you have to go out with a spade, plunge it ruthlessly into the water, and cut off the roots, feeling like a murderer. Ultra-sensitive persons, while engaged in such operations, might feel inclined to close the eyes. I keep mine open, with an effort. After all, one might bisect a goldfish.

Which is all I shall have to say about water gardens. It will have no effect on anybody whatsoever. Nobody, but nobody, will be tempted even to fill a bucket of water, sink it in the lawn, and float a sprig of watercress on top of it. One of the things one learns, as one grows older, is that nobody ever listens. No, I should not have written that. A few people do listen sometimes, but they are very few. However, there *might* be one or two strange creatures, covered with bind-weed, lurking in faded parlours in darkest Cumberland, who *might* feel, after all this, that there was something to be said for a water garden. They *might* feel that it was worthwhile to dig a hole in the lawn, and by doing so, to create a whole world of magic and delight. But I very much doubt it. The vast majority of mankind prefer to sit in a deck-chair in the middle of an empty lawn, contemplating the plantains.

CHAPTER FOURTEEN

FRAGRANCE

IT will be generally conceded, in respectable society, that there must be something radically wrong with gentlemen who like scent. Gentlemen—real gentlemen, like Mr Evelyn Waugh—should be unaware of it. They may have a palate for wine, or an ear for music, or an appreciation of the ballet, but scent . . . no. Maybe there could be certain exceptional circumstances in which a touch of eau-de-Cologne, furtively applied to the extreme tip of the handkerchief projecting from the breast-pocket, might not completely wreck their social chances. But it is a very tentative maybe. I would not know. I must write to Mr Waugh about it.

To myself, scent is among the minor, but keener, pleasures of life. After all, one is an animal, and if one could switch the clock back a few million years, one would probably find oneself sniffing around the most unexpected places, covered with fur, and snorting. Mr Waugh, too. Whether the present activities of mankind are to be regarded as an advance on such conduct is a matter of opinion. I know mine.

There are melancholy scents—pear blossom that carries with it a feeling that youth is all too transient; there are gay scents, such as the laughing perfume of vine blossoms, which Bacon described as the sweetest of all the garden's essences. There are feminine scents—some of them, like gardenias, so intensely feminine that they are almost embarrassing. And there are masculine scents—moss, bergamot, wood smoke, new-mown hay, and certain vegetables, such as the velvety inside of young broad beans. These, not unnaturally, have a special appeal to myself. Let us consider some of these which are not too widely known.

We might begin with the mints, because in these we discover scents which most people do not associate with mint at all: peppermint, apple, and eau-de-Cologne. This is not imagination; if you crush them in your fingers and give them to a friend to smell, he will immediately recognize the flavour. Moreover, the Corsican mint, *Mentha requienii*, provides us with an opportunity to indulge a charming fancy . . . a scented lawn. Sown very lightly, so that it blends into the grass without making dark patches, it will give out a delicious tang when you are mowing the lawn. In my present garden I have not yet sown any; there have been too many other things to do; but at Merry Hall, where the lawns were larger, there were always stray patches of peppermint, which appealed not only to myself but also to the cats, who used to sniff them out and lie down on them, with evident delight. Afterwards, when they came to sit on one's lap, their fur smelt most agreeable. There may be some eccentric people who do not like peppermint-scented cats, but it will surely be generally agreed that they are preferable to peppermint-scented people.

Apart from its scent, this mint, with its tiny flowers and its creeping habit, is ideal for filling chinks in crazy pavements. There must be something masochistic about it, for it positively asks to be trodden on. If you go in for it, you might plant it next to the apple-scented variety, whose pretty leaves are striped with silver. It is not my fault that this little charmer bears the elephantine name of *Mentha rotundifolia variegata*.

The usual sordid Practical Notes, which could not be simpler, are in the appendix.

*   *   *

Scented plants, I think, should be disposed strategically. By which I mean that there should be something at the front door, to calm one's goings out and comfort one's comings in, and something at the end of the lawn to sniff, and crunch, and talk about.

Such as the lemon verbena in my porch. This is, quite definitely, one of the major consolations of life. One is going out to some ghastly business lunch, at which fiendish suggestions will be made by hard-faced American editors. Such as that one should instantly provide them with five thousand words on the Night Thoughts of Lord Snowdon—which would be formidable indeed. The lemon verbena somehow gives one strength to grapple with the situation. And even if things go wrong, and one finds oneself committed to two thousand words on the Day Thoughts of Princess Alexandra —a comparatively dainty assignment—the lemon verbena is there to refresh one, to remind one that things might be worse, and that even the great Balzac spilled a large amount of his genius on the compilation of advertisements for ladies' underwear.

Back to the lemon verbena—*Lippia citriodora*, if we are being formal. It smells of lemon-peel, honey, and the south wind, and I have wasted thousands of words in trying to convince people that it is hardier than its reputation. I know of a lippia that yearly attains a height of five feet in a back-yard not a mile from Glasgow Central Station, which can scarcely be described as a tropical playground. The one vital —repeat vital—requirement is winter protection of the roots. These are fibrous and very near the surface, and you must remember that frost digs its sharp claws deep—maybe nine inches down. You can guard against that by a blanket of bracken or dry leaves or even a cloche.

Here is a sort of personal pot-pourri of some of the scented plants in my own garden, selected at random, as they come to mind. Most of them have a somewhat masculine flavour, but the first is very feminine indeed. It is a charming little Chinese shrub, with small white flowers rather like a jasmine. It is called:

Osmanthus delavayi. To describe the scent of this flower one must lapse into commercial French. 'Troublant . . . sedui-sant . . . mysterieux'—that sort of thing. One has only to sniff it to recall the stock adjectives of the Parisian perfume manufacturers, and to conjure up a vision of the swelling bosoms of the young ladies whose love-life, we are assured, it is designed to stimulate. I have a special tenderness for these young ladies, and at times a certain pity for them; it must be exhausting to spend one's life with perpetually parted nostrils, staggering through a scented mist towards a divan whose springs are probably broken. And I should hate to remind them that their troubling, seductive and mysterious mixtures are not, in fact, mysterious at all. They begin with a basis of neat skunk, and the chemicals that are added afterwards are no more mysterious than the ingredients for a common aperient.

None of this detracts from the special deliciousness of the osmanthus, as you will discover if you are wise enough to plant it.

The Peppermint Geranium, Pelargonium tomentosum. I introduce this plant rather hastily, as an earthy antidote to the exotic fumes of the osmanthus. With the exception of the ivy varieties all the geraniums are, of course, delicately scented, if not in the flowers, in the leaves. But there is nothing delicate about the peppermint geranium; it is just plain peppermint cream. Which is why children make a bee-line for it if you are rash enough to admit them to the cold greenhouse where it belongs. The flowers are negligible, but the leaves have great beauty—grey-green, downy, and smooth as the paws of a kitten.

Incidentally, one of the most endearing pictures in the panorama of my domestic life will always be the sight of Gaskin walking across the lawn, on summer mornings, in order to pick a handful of these geranium leaves to flavour iced peppermint jelly.

Lovage. I warned you that our list would be compiled at random. This plant is introduced here, because in the last paragraph we seemed to have strayed for a moment from the garden into the kitchen.

Never mind. If this somewhat arbitrary diversion is a means of bringing lovage into your life, you will never regret it.

Lovage is not so much a scent as a savour, and the taste is very easy to describe; it is exactly like smoked celery. Ask anybody to bite it and he will immediately say 'celery'; then he thinks again and says: 'but there's something else'. He usually gets the smoke ingredient a few moments later.

Why is this plant, which offers us a taste unique in nature, unknown to the great majority of gardeners and cooks? Heaven knows, it has a long enough history; it was originally brought over by the Romans and I have been told that at one time it grew wild in the Hebrides, which is a proof of its toughness. One would have thought that it would have been extolled by every herbalist who ever lived, but the only reference to it that I have been able to discover was made nearly four centuries ago, when Thomas Hyll, in *The Gardener's Labyrinth* (1577) wrote that: 'This herbe for hys sweete savour is used in bathe.' After this pleasing but not very illuminating comment silence descends on the lovage, until it is broken by three not very enthusiastic lines in Constance Spry's cookery book.

I cannot understand this neglect, for when one uses lovage in a salad it invariably steals the show. Try this experiment. Ask some people to luncheon, preferably female. Serve them with a salad flavoured with lovage. Don't make a fuss about it; don't draw attention to it; don't say, casually, that this is one of the *spécialités de la maison*—not that one is in the habit of saying such things, but you know what I mean. Just put the salad before them, and let it work its spell. You will be fascinated by what happens. Crisp leaves are put into dainty mouths and then the dainty mouths snap, and the eyes glint, and the female brain works, and says to itself: 'We must know more about this, we must get the secret out of him, and will get it in private, because darling Ada opposite, though we all dote on her, is not really subtle enough for these delights.' But meanwhile, darling Ada opposite is also snapping and glinting, and making similar resolves. All of which adds up to a pleasing conclusion after luncheon, when one is drawn aside by one or other of the ladies, and dulcet enquiries are made, with many furtive glances over the shoulder, as to the precise nature of the flavour which we have recently been sampling.

Well, now the secret is out. The answer is lovage. The Latin name is *Ligusticum scoticum* and there are still a few enterprising nurserymen who supply seeds. (See appendix.) But if you decide to grow it you had better write early; after these transports it may be sold out.

And now we must leave the kitchen and go back to the garden.

The Scented Poplar. In every garden that I have ever owned, until now, I have planted a scented poplar, *Populus trichocarpa*, but there is no room for one in my present acre; it grows like a beanstalk and has very greedy roots. I feel the loss of it all through the first three weeks of May, after which the scent begins to fade. But when the sticky buds are unfolding and the sun strikes the pale green leaves—which are most delicately veined on the underside—the scent is of an exquisite sweetness, like incense with a faint hint of lemon. Moreover, this scent has an astonishing 'spread'; in my former garden at Merry Hall it used to find its way through the whole orchard and drift over the lane. Indeed I know of only one other fragrance with this same love of travelling, and that is the wood smoke made by a fire of old laurel logs. On a still day, with a very gentle breeze, you can smell it across the fields at a distance of over a mile.

Rosemary. I mention this rather obvious choice because I suspect that most people, when they speak of rosemary, are only aware of the old-fashioned variety which one finds in so many cottage gardens. This is certainly charming enough, and I should hate to be without it—particularly in the winter, when one can make charming little arrangements of the leaves, all by themselves, in small vases. After a few days the stems have an engaging habit of curling upwards and inwards. When this happens you take them out of the vase and rearrange them the other way around, so that they give a weeping effect. They look faintly surprised by such treatment, but extremely elegant.

However, there are all sorts of rosemaries, some of them with such fancy names and descriptions that one is inclined to view them with mistrust. I speak only of those that I know from personal experience. These include:

Rosmarinus officinalis angustifolius. This lovely thing comes from Corsica, and in the bright blue of its flowers there is a glint of the seas that tumble round that somewhat over-scorched pleasance. The leaves are thin and feathery, and if you have the right place for it—well drained, in full sun, on not too rich a soil—it *may* develop into a grand shrub that deserves to be spotlit. I have written the word 'may' in italics because if it does not like you it *may* also give a vivid impersonation of a clump of starved asparagus fern. This happened in my garden for six years, before I found the right place.

There are several other shades of rosemary; white and pink (*albus* and *rosea*), and an especially brilliant variety, Tuscan Blue—though this is too tender for my liking. For the gardener who has space for only one variety I would recommend Severn Seas, not only for the brightness of its flowers and the sweetness of its scent, but because the branches have a tendency to droop and because it doesn't get straggly.

PRACTICAL NOTE

Rosemary is very difficult to grow from seed; it is better to buy plants, which are easy to come by at 3s. 6d. upwards.

NOT SO PRACTICAL NOTE

Rosemary, like all things scented, has a fragrant history. (Which suggests that of all the senses, the most evocative is the sense of smell—tarred string and seaside holidays in Cornwall, the lid of an old cedar-wood box and the memory of ancient cigars drifting through departed dining-rooms.) For this reason, maybe, it appealed to Sir Thomas More, who made an art of friendship, and grew it 'not onlie because my bees love it, but because it is the herb sacred to remembrance and to friendship, whence a sprig of it hath a dumb language'.

Winter Scents. Odd as it may seem, winter brings some of the sweetest scents to the garden. And even odder, unless you have a very large garden, I would not recommend you to grow quite a number of the plants which produce these scents—for example the drenchingly sweet winter honeysuckle (*Lonicera fragrantissima*). In the old days, when I had a large orchard, I used to extol this shrub, because it really *is* a honeysuckle, and it really *does* flower, intermittently, from Christmas onwards. But in a small garden it is far too straggly, and when the flowers are over you will probably decide that it is rather a bore. The same applies to the wintersweet (*Chimonanthus fragrans*), whose flowers look like yellow wax insects and blossom on the bare stem in mid-January. If you have a huge kitchen garden with a sunny, out-of-the-way corner you should certainly have it, for a few sprays will scent a whole room with an enchanting fragrance that smells of peaches and vanilla. Otherwise, eschew it, for all through the summer it looks decidedly drab.

But even in the smallest garden there is room for the following:

Daphne mezereum. This is a 'must'. It very seldom grows to a height of more than three feet, and even in its first year the leafless sprays are covered with strongly-scented flowers that come in white and rose pink and pale purple. As I seem to be in a severely practical mood I must mention one drawback to which the nurseryman seldom, if ever, calls attention—it has a short life span of only about seven years. Just when you have come to regard it as an established friend, it suddenly gives up the ghost. Why this should be I do not know. But it is not all that important, for daphnes produce abundant seed, so that you can always have a little family of young ones to carry on when the parents have gone.

Viburnum fragans. This is an extraordinary shrub, for you can never be quite sure when it is going to flower. However, it will almost certainly produce its first blossoms in November. Then after a fortnight or so it may decide to shut up shop, only to come out in a mass of blossom with the first January sunshine. On the other hand, it may do nothing at all till the end of February. All that one can guarantee is that it will produce *some* flowers during the hardest winter, and very welcome they are, waxy, pinkish white and in fragrance reminiscent of the rind of a melon. They have only one disadvantage; they are inclined to drop when you bring them indoors, so that if you are very fussy about furniture polish you will have to be careful where you stand them.

Wild White Violets. Here we switch—not for the first time!—from horticulture to autobiography. In every garden I have ever owned there has been a clump of wild white violets. These are the direct descendants of some roots which I dug up from the steep red banks of the Devonshire lanes, when I was a small boy going for walks with my governess, Miss Herridge. (In later years, I came to write of her, under the name of Miss Hazlitt, in the trilogy which began with *Down the Garden Path.*) Miss Herridge was an ideal guide for a small boy making his first wide-eyed discoveries in the magic landscapes of nature; she was the daughter of a distinguished botanist, and though she shared my ecstasies she tempered them with knowledge and restrained them with discipline, forbidding me, for example, to pick bunches of the wild winter heliotrope until I had written out its Latin name, *Petasites fragrans*, fifty times in a clear round script. Then, and not till then, was I allowed to gather this humble but exotically fragrant flower, and bring it home, and set it in the centre of the tea-table, and gloat over it while we ate our scones and mulberry jam. Incidentally, that distinguished gardener Sir Compton Mackenzie has often sternly reproved me for recommending people to plant winter heliotrope in their gardens, for it swiftly develops into a rampant weed which is impossible to eradicate. If I were rewriting *Down the Garden Path*, I would certainly point out this drawback, but I still think that anybody who has an odd corner in an orchard or a rough bank safely out of reach of the border is foolish to deny himself its mid-winter fragrance of cloves and honey. It is only recently that the petasites has fallen into such ill repute; when it was introduced from Italy early in the nineteenth century it was esteemed as a plant for growing in pots—and maybe a pot is the best place for it.

But it is the scent of the wild white violets that recalls Miss Herridge most vividly to me, as we went for our walks through the lanes that stretch round the village of Cockington—lanes that in those days were a treasury of wild flowers. Most of the names of those flowers have long ago faded from my memory, but I can still see the pink Ragged Robbins, looking up through the feathery flowers of Queen Anne's Lace, like the rosy cheeks of a young girl through a bridal veil. I can still taste the acid-drop tang of the leaves of the wood sorrel, which I only munched in secret because it was 'bad for the teeth'. And feel the thin, cool skin of the corn-wort, which was supposed to cure corns, and remember longing for the day when I could grow a corn myself, in order to test its magic properties. Well, that day has come and gone. And what all this has got to do with scent I really do not know. But perhaps, in some of the foregoing fragrances that I have tried to evoke, you may find an echo of some of your own memories, or a hint that will sweeten the memories that are still to come.

Lunaria annua monstruosum

Helichrysum

Physalis franchetii

CHAPTER FIFTEEN

A TOUCH OF ARTIFICE

Artificial flowers, that never bloomed in any spring . . .
I can't afford the real thing,
They're all I've got to wear.
Artificial flowers! Although these snowdrops look
  quite sweet
They smell offensive in the heat
It's very hard to bear.

That was the opening of a song that I composed, quite a while ago, for a revue. Now and again it still echoes over the radio, in the darkest hours before the dawn, bringing me in an annual income of several shillings. You may gather from it that I do not care for artificial flowers. This would be an understatement; I should like to make a bonfire of the whole hard, dusty, chemically-coloured collection. Better a withered dandelion in a jam pot than these bogus monstrosities.

So why write in praise of the *Helichrysum*—the familiar 'everlasting' flower, with its crisp dry petals of white and cherry and lemon and magenta? Surely these are 'artificial'? And I suppose the answer would be yes, if you have only seen them in the shops at Christmas time, packed tightly together like bonbons in a basket, wedged between bottles of bath-salts and jars of ginger. In such circumstances it is hard to believe that they ever had a place in a garden— that they thrilled to the rain and nodded in the wind, exchanging confidences with their next-door neighbours. Perhaps, being immortal, they do no such things; perhaps they feel superior, saying to themselves: 'Lupins may come and lupins may go, but we go on for ever.' However, whimsy is just round the corner, so we had better not pursue that line of thought.

And yet, I should like to pursue it. For if I had the habit of making speeches to flowers—which, to be quite honest and above-board, I have—I should say to them: 'Let's have a little less of this nonsense about going on for ever. Don't be greedy. Be grateful that you are lovely for a summer and don't try to cling to that loveliness, like professional beauties who refuse to grow old.'

It is not the fault of the flowers, of course. It is the fault of the people who refuse to treat them as flowers. Hardly ever does one see them massed in the August border, where they outshine the petunias and the summer chrysanthemums and blaze more brightly than the zinnias. That is how to treat them, and when the year is dying, root them up and cast them away. Mortal or immortal, they have served their purpose.

PRACTICAL NOTE

Everlasting flowers are best grown from seed. The directions will be on the packet. I recommend the large double mixed variety, which goes by the name of *Helichrysum bracteatum monstrosum.*

*　　*　　*

But there are one or two 'everlasting' flowers which I *do* keep, and dry and use for decoration, simply because their appearance is so absurdly artificial that they look more at home indoors than out, as though Nature had designed them in a mood of super-sophistication. Of these flowers I would put on the top of the list the winter cherry or—to give it the name which really suits it best—the Chinese Lantern.

In case you do not know this old-fashioned treasure, which has suffered a sad neglect in recent years, it is very easy to describe because it looks exactly like its name. The flowers are insignificant but the berries, which ripen from October onwards, are spectacular. Each stem—and the stems often reach a height of four feet—is hung with quantities of brilliant scarlet-orange calyces, which seem to be made out of dyed paper. They are about the size of a small tangerine. If you split open a calyx you will find inside it something like a cherry, which you can eat if you have a morbidly curious temperament. But I don't advise it.

Why has this amiable plant fallen out of favour? For Christmas decoration it is ideal, and though it may not have the sentimental associations of holly it is far showier, and it does not scratch. Moreover, it has a pleasant drooping habit so that you can drape it round pictures, or contrive little cascades of it to tumble down the banisters.

I do more than this. I cut all the leaves off and gild the seed pods, setting them in the Regency wine-cooler in front of the old Chippendale mirror, where they look unbelievably opulent. You may say that this procedure is inconsistent with a dislike of artificial flowers; my excuse must be that Nature made them so 'artificial' that whatever you may do to them will not change their essential character. You may also suggest that it is vulgar to speak of 'opulence' in connection with floral decoration. I do not find it so. Sometimes, in the festive season, I press my nose against the windows of expensive florists' shops and study their glittering arrangements of frosted leaves, silvered berries and spangled branches. I also study the prices. Half a guinea a spray, in many cases. But not nearly as grand nor as glittering as my Chinese lanterns, which only cost me a half-crown bottle of gold paint from Woolworth's.

PRACTICAL NOTE

The botanical name of the Chinese Lantern is *Physalis franchetii*. Details of nurserymen who supply it, in seed or plant form, in the appendix.

It could hardly be easier to grow; indeed, once it is established it strikes out so vigorously that you will have to start pulling up the roots that have strayed too far. For this reason, and also because you grow it primarily for cutting, it should never be planted in front of the border. Let it ramp away at the back, fighting its way towards the sunshine, undeterred by the roots of the surrounding trees.

*   *   *

And now, a word in praise of Honesty. The curious plant that is known, almost exclusively, for its paper-thin oval seed-pods, the colour of old ivory, pods that recall the faded counters in a forgotten game of chance.

Most people 'of a certain age' who were raised in the impoverished middle classes—which includes me—associate Honesty with the lodgings of seaside landladies. Down to the sea we used to go, not in ships but in second-class railway compartments, for that magical fortnight in September . . . to Worthing, to Torquay, to Penzance. Along the seafront we trundled, in ancient Daimlers, with the luggage strapped to the back. And we rang the bell at 'Seaview' and trooped upstairs and inspected our quarters. And there, quite inevitably, on the upright piano, was the vase of Honesty. Stuck in a glazed green vase, covered with dust, casting its sad shadow over a fly-blown family group. The very sight of it used to make me shiver—but then, as a child, I had rather more than my share to shiver about.

A great deal of water had to flow under a great many bridges before I realized that those seed-pods were not skeletons at the family feast, that they had their own delightful decorative purposes—set in a white bowl against a white wall, with the light of a white candle flecking them to silver. And even more rivers had to run before I realized that Honesty was even more desirable in life than in death, because of the beauty of its purplish flower. It stands very upright, and is of the most candid countenance. When I first opened my garden to the public hardly anybody seemed to recognize it when they saw the little drift that has seeded itself under the eucalyptus. When I told them that it was Honesty some of them—particularly those square, bulldog women who walk across a lawn as though they were treading in the turf—

became quite aggressive. Honesty? It was no such thing. *They* knew what Honesty was . . . implying, very definitely, that I didn't, in any sense of the word. So in the end I decided that it would be wiser to answer in Latin. '*Lunaria annua monstruosum*', I retorted. Which put them briskly in their places.

All yours for a shilling a packet. Incidentally, once your Honesty is well established, it will begin to seed itself in the most obliging way.

*   *   *

There is only the slenderest of links to this chapter—the word artifice. And now, even this link seems to have snapped, for we are about to switch to tulips, in particular, to the glorious varieties gathered under the single name of Rembrandt. Are these really so 'artificial'? Maybe not; but I have to write about them somewhere or this book would not be complete. They are the only sort—or very nearly the only sort—that I ever grow.

True, this concentration on the Rembrandts is due, in some degree, to lack of space. If one had rolling acres obviously one would buy tulips by the thousands and tens of thousands, in all their diversity of grace and elegance. Even as things are, I usually manage to find space for a few dozen of the new arrivals that burst upon us every year at the Chelsea Show, such as the dazzling Violet Queen, which is to the average tulip what a super-bedizened film star is to the average woman. Oh, those Chelsea Shows, and the tortures to which they subject the owners of small gardens! One wanders round in a state of mounting palpitation, ordering dozens of this and hundreds of that, to the great satisfaction of the bronzed young men behind the ropes. Then one goes home, and looks around, and there is nowhere, but nowhere, to put them. When they arrive, one has to give them away, which may be pleasant, but is extremely expensive.

This is why, when I think of tulips, I think almost exclusively in terms of Rembrandts. If you are restricted to one variety there is nothing to compare with them.

The name explains itself; they are the tulips that still delight us in the old Dutch flower pictures, striped in all the colours of the rainbow, gay, sombre, daring, modest, none matching the other.

Of all flowers, with the exception of the rose, the tulip has the most colourful history. It began to delight the world in the middle of the sixteenth century; a hundred years later men were bidding for parcels of the bulbs with the same excitement as they bid for shares on the stock exchange; and in France, when the first houses of fashion were establishing themselves, the vase of tulips on the golden staircase was a foretaste of delights to come and always, remember, they were Rembrandts.

For once in a way, the description in the catalogues does not exceed the reality. I quote from one of them:

It embraces the shades of striped and flaked scarlet on a white ground; orange, brown and black feathering on a white ground. If cut, these tulips create a historical and yet modern effect.

The precise meaning of the last sentence evades me, but you will get the general idea.

But Rembrandt tulips grace very few English gardens, and I have yet to see them in an English park. Darwins, yes, and the early singles, and the late doubles—(those horrid pink and white things that remind one of the iced lollipops that are compulsory eating, at all times of the day, for the modern infant). But the lovely Rembrandts, no. Please give them a thought.

PRACTICAL NOTE

Rembrandts are not expensive, as tulips go. Fifty shillings per hundred. Moreover, they have a longer life than most other varieties. You can leave them in the ground for several years, and though they gradually diminish in size, they keep their character and their beauty. After the fifth year you will probably want to lift them and replant with new stock. Even so, I would not throw them away. They will continue to enchant you in a little corner of the kitchen garden, in a slow diminuendo of blossom through the years.

Rembrandt Tulips

CHAPTER SIXTEEN

CLIMBING HIGH

I<small>F</small> one holds forth about gardening in public, one must be prepared for a varied and often bizarre correspondence.

People write from Jamaica, enclosing seeds of flowers which quite obviously need a constant temperature of ninety in the shade, suggesting that one plants them in darkest Surrey, and adding that they would be pleased to receive coloured photographs of 'same'.

Others send photographs of back-yards, often with a pussy on the wall—I like that part of the photograph best—demanding to know what they shall do about it. Shall they put up a trellis? If so what shall they grow on it? And if they grow something on it, will there be any legal complications with the lady next door, who has no soul coupled with arthritis.

Then there are the people who send little tins. My heart sinks when I see them, wrapped in damp brown paper, insufficiently stamped. Almost always they contain one of two things. Either it will be a flower to be identified, or a bunch to put on my desk—dog violets, wild cyclamen, early honey-suckle from the Devon woods. Only a man with a heart of stone could remain untouched by these little offerings and only a pompous bore would not be flattered by them. Un-happily, in nineteen cases out of twenty, they arrive in a state of decay beyond revival and have to be thrown straight away.

So what does one do? Write and tell the truth? But how, and in what words? It is not easy to look a gift horse in the mouth, particularly if it is lying dead on the compost heap. Write and tell a lie? Say that the flowers came in perfect condition and are at this very moment delighting the eye? But if we do that, the parcels will continue to arrive, more stamps will be wasted at the other end, and eventually we shall run out of words.

The worst parcels are those containing fruit, which quite invariably arrives in a state of gruesome putrefaction.

I seem to be expending a lot of space on this problem, but it is not academic. We all have the dear old friend or relation who, having spent hours gathering the best plums and peaches in her kitchen garden, wraps them up in tissue paper, and dispatches them with a charming note saying that they will be 'so different from the sort that one buys in the shops'. Which, indeed, is all too true. For the plums and peaches have turned, in transit, into a terrifying compote of diseased vegetable matter.

Long years of experience have convinced me that the wisest thing is to be quite honest from the word one. Write back and say that one is touched beyond measure, that the flowers must indeed have been beautiful and the peaches superb, but unfortunately etc. etc. One might also add some-thing about the dilatory habits of the Post Office.

After this it may seem strange if I express the hope that I may one day hear again from the old gentleman who used to send me the tin of white Parma violets from Teignmouth. They always arrived as if they had just been picked, and I should like to think that he is still with us and that the violets are still flowering for him—and maybe for me!

*　　*　　*

But we were supposed to be talking of the letters received by gardening correspondents. One of them lies before me now—the one which gave me the title for this chapter.

> I am an old age pensioner with a mother—eighty-six —who is bedridden and never comes downstairs. We live in a new house with bare walls and I do so long for her to have some flowers to look in through her window, particularly at this time of year. (October 15th.) All her life, till we came here, she had flowers looking in at her window, she said she liked them best because they seem- ed so friendly. But we have very little money to spare so if it could be something I could grow from seed so much the better. And it would have to be quick too—at her age. Please, is there anything you can recommend?

It happened that I was temporarily bedridden myself when I received this letter. When I had read it, I looked out of my own window, which is about fifteen feet from the ground, and I saw the answer.

It was a flower shaped like a dark purple Canterbury bell, tapping against the lowest pane of the glass. I sowed it this spring in a cold greenhouse (a sheet of glass over a box on a

179

window-ledge would probably do as well). And in spite of a wet-dreary summer it had ramped away up the wall, and now here it was, looking in through the window, cheering me up.

Its name? Cathedral Bells is one of them. Cups and Saucers is another. Fairy Lanterns is yet another, and very pretty they all are. But I am afraid that sooner or later we shall have to face the grim truth—*Cobaea scandens*.

Does this flower—which really is an enchanting conceit of Nature—meet our old lady's requirements? I think it does, for three reasons.

Firstly, it is cheap. From a 1s. 6d. packet of seed I raised two dozen creepers, most of which had to be given away, for lack of wall space.

Secondly, it is self-supporting; it does not need a trellis or wires or nails. Our old ladies won't have to go through all that business of borrowing ladders and risking their necks. It is equipped with sturdy tentacles, which find their way into the smallest cracks and crevices, in the manner of a Virginia creeper. All the same, in a windy district, it would probably be grateful for the encouragement of a nail or two, here and there.

And thirdly? It really does all this in a single year; you can almost watch it grow. My own is planted on a wall facing east, and it has had little sunshine and an inordinate amount of buffeting by the winds and the rains. I almost dread to think what it would do in a normal summer.

PRACTICAL NOTE

When you sow the seeds, sow them *on edge*. They are quite large and flat, so that this is not difficult. It is merely a matter of a little patience. Don't ask me why you have to adopt this

Abutilon milleri

Clematis tangutica

Cobaea scandens

Clematis Nellie Moser

strange procedure; the ways of Nature are unfathomable.

*   *   *

Of the more familiar 'high climbers'—the Virginia creepers, the wistarias, the ivies, the *Clematis montana* and *jackmanii*—it would be superfluous to write in these pages; one must assume that there is nothing more to be said about them. We are in search of rarer treasures.

However, in passing, I would like to make a mild protest at the enormous amount of wall space wasted in this country; it must run to many thousands of square miles. Why these vast areas of bleak brick, which might so easily be transformed into avenues of blossom? Even people with nice little well-tended gardens in the suburbs usually leave three of their four walls naked. Why? It cannot be because they admire the architecture; they cannot, surely, wish to wander round the lawn in a trance of delight induced by a façade of stockbroker Tudor? No. This nakedness—like many other forms of nakedness—must be the result either of ignorance or laziness. Probably the former. If we were to ask the lady of the house why the back of her dwelling was a mass of bare ugly pipes and why her tool-shed was a corrugated eyesore she would probably reply with a lot of nonsense about the wall never getting any sun or the tool-shed being surrounded by concrete. Neither of these considerations is of the least importance.

And yet, these wicked slothful women—forgive me, but I do feel rather strongly about it—are the very same women who will spend hours in the soft furnishing departments, squinting at a piece of brocade to match up with the bedroom curtains, under a macabre contraption that is supposed to simulate daylight but, in fact, tinges everything that it illuminates with a form of moonlight madness.

If you really feel—as I hope you may—that you might prefer leaves and flowers to bare brick, wherever you may live, north or south, town or country, your best plan is to get hold of a nurseryman's catalogue and turn up the section devoted to 'Climbers and Wall Shrubs'. There you will find —unless you happen to have settled on an ice-floe—something which fits *every* situation. Climbers for north walls, south walls, any sort of wall. Climbers that will grow in tubs, or out of a hole in the concrete. Climbers that will shake off the soot and the stench of the district railway. You will find these brave and wonderful creatures at an average price of 8s. 6d., with full cultural directions. You will also find in these catalogues some of the best prose that is now being written in the English language. Tough and gnarled and earthy, but touched, at times, with poetry.

A short list of the best of these catalogues is included in the appendix.

*   *   *

Where were we?

'In search of rarer treasures.'

Very well. Here is one, which you will find in very few gardens indeed, of such spectacular beauty that when I 'open to the public' there is always a little crowd round it, standing and staring. The name, *Abutilon milleri*.

In spite of its unusual appearance—or maybe because of it —this abutilon is very easy to describe. Let us begin with the leaves, which are soft and supple, shaped like a large ivy. Each leaf carries a design which immediately recalls an abstract painting of the Cubist period; indeed if you were to photograph one of them, enlarge it and frame it, you could pass it off as a Picasso, *circa* 1910. These designs are formed by straight lines ruled in dark green, creating a criss-cross of squares and oblongs in jade, sea-green, emerald and pale yellow. No design is duplicated; each is an individual master-piece; and one leaf, set in a wine glass and placed on a bare table, should give a sensible person enough to meditate upon for at least an hour.

Now for the flowers. These again are easy to describe because no other flower in Nature—at least, none that I know of—has the same colour combination. Chocolate and pale, tangerine is how I would classify them. The flowers are about the size of the end of one's thumb. In bud they look exactly like chocolate drops; then they open out into exquisite bells, with the pale yellow petals emerging from a chocolate calyx. Inside, hanging like the clapper of a church bell, is yet another delight, a bunch of stamens richly dusted with gold. I have just been out to examine my own abutilon, which is a mass of blossom covering about six square feet of wall space, in order to check this description, word by word. I found nothing to alter in it.

And now—the snag! This abutilon is on the tender side; it is one of those maddening creatures which carries an asterisk in the catalogues, indicating that it is 'not suitable for exposed positions in any but the mildest localities though in most districts it is hardy on a wall'. Admittedly, my own is in the cold greenhouse. But here is a word of comfort. Last winter, by some mischance, the door of the greenhouse was kept wide open throughout three days of severe frost, and though a great deal of damage was done, even to plants like semi-hardy fuschias, the abutilon did not turn a hair. So I think we may assume that it is tougher than its reputation. In any case, it is of such unique and startling loveliness, and it flowers so freely and for so long a period, that it is well worth a try.

PRACTICAL NOTE

There are several species of abutilon, but none quite as fine as the *milleri*, though all have the same strange beauty of leaf. They are not in very wide supply. If you are unable to obtain a *milleri*, the next best is *megapotamicum variegatum*, the leaves of which are flecked with gold.

*   *   *

The Clematis Family

In the introduction to this book I gave notice that I might be coming into rather sharp conflict with the 'experts', and this is one of the occasions when I do so. Not from any foolish desire to claim omniscience but because—well, because experts can sometimes be wrong and amateurs can some- times be right. After gardening for thirty years as an amateur, it is surely inevitable that there must have been occasions when one has stumbled on to something which does not tally with 'what it says in the book'. The greatest service of the amateur in the art of gardening—or indeed in any of the arts —is that he does things wrong, either from courage, obstinacy or sheer stupidity. He breaks rules right and left, planting things in the wrong soil at the wrong time of the year in the wrong aspect. And usually, we must admit, the result is disastrous. But not always.

So it has been with my experience of the clematis family. I have consistently broken so many rules, with such marked success, that I have no hesitation whatsoever in stating that most of the experts are talking through their hats.

For example, all the experts, without exception, insist that their roots must be kept in the shade. If this is so, how does it happen that on my own west wall, in full sunshine, with no root protection whatsoever, except for the occasional shadow of a transitory cat, I have three sorts—*montana*, Nellie Moser and *jackmanii*—which flourish so lustily and flower so freely that by July they are beginning to cover up my bedroom window with a waving curtain of colour? If any expert doubts this, he is welcome to come and look at them and— I hope—admit the error of his ways.

Again, apart from this shaded root illusion, we are told that the majority of the family demand full sunshine. To which the simple answer is, they don't. True, they will not like a damp north wall, but you can plant varieties like *jackmanii* at the root of gnarled old fruit trees whose leaves deny them any hint of sunshine. They will fight their way up the trunk and along the branches towards the light, and kindle their purple lamps in time to celebrate the harvesting of the fruit.

Finally, pruning.

Here the conflict becomes violent. On my desk lies the catalogue of one of the largest clematis growers in the country. It is prefaced with three pages of 'cultural hints', in which the importance of drastic pruning is emphasized again and again. With some varieties it is even recommended that the plants should be cut down every year to the level of the soil.

To which I can only reply that I have never pruned a clematis in my life. True, I have trained them and occasionally cut out some of the dead wood, but all that hacking and chopping and starting all over again—never. And yet, from mid-April to early August, I have as fine a display of clematis as you will find in any 'expert's' nursery. Why?

There is nothing magic about my garden and—contrary to general belief—there are no fairies at the bottom of it. So why? Is it not possible that the 'experts' are wrong?

Here I would like to call in evidence of one of the grandest old gardeners who ever lived, the late Lord Aberconway, who was for so many years President of the Royal Horticultural Society. Once, on a walk through the paradise gardens of Bodnant, he paused in front of a clematis—I forget the variety—that was giving a static firework display of blossom against an old brick wall. I asked him when it had last been pruned. 'Never. There is one thing to remember about clematis,' he said. 'If they like you, leave them alone.' An axiom which, I feel dimly, might also have some application to one's dealings with one's fellow men.

So much for this 'expert' business, which as I am sure you will agree, was beginning to get rather boring.

What about the varieties you should choose? In my own garden I would have fifty, if there were space for them; as things are, I have only nine. And of these, I present for your attention, only one, the *Clematis tangutica*.

If I describe this lovely and seldom grown clematis as a chime of golden bells it is not because the phrase is pretty but because it precisely conveys the quality of the blossom. We do not usually associate the clematis with a campanular formation, but in this singular variety the flowers hang as though suspended in a floral belfry, and with the wind their yellow petals catch a metallic gleam.

When they fall, the gold gives place to silver, for of all the clematis family this has the brightest seed heads. Sheer silver, and—in spite of their delicate appearance, which makes them look as though they had been woven by a tribe of exceptionally aesthetic spiders—surprisingly tough. So tough, indeed, that in the autumn you can gather bunches of them and enhance their brilliance by speckling them with silver paint for your Christmas decorations. Never a seed will drop and the result is not nearly so horrid as it sounds.

PRACTICAL NOTE

My own *tangutica* is planted at the foot of a wall thickly covered with firethorn which affords it an ideal support—the pale melody of the blossom dancing against the dark underbass of the leaves. In the course of three years it has climbed to a height of nearly twenty feet, and the only reason it does not climb any higher is because there is nothing left for it to climb up. I have never cut it nor manured it, nor tied it, nor watered it, nor given it anything—but love. Of which, admittedly, it has had a great deal.

Although *Clematis tangutica* is grown so rarely, it is in abundant supply and it is not expensive; the average cost at most nurseries is 7s. 6d. As all clematis are grown in pots it may be safely planted at any time from September to early May.

Odontoglossum crispum

Pleione Formosana

Rowan

Clerodendrum
trichotomum

CHAPTER SEVENTEEN

THE WOMAN'S TOUCH

WOMEN gardeners are mysterious creatures. When they are old, admittedly, they are wonderful. You only have to go to the Chelsea Show to prove this—or, indeed, to any of the big shows which enliven London throughout the year. Up they flock from the country in their thousands, with limbs like twisted roots, and keen, wise old faces that might have been carved from the bark of ancient trees. They hobble round with astonishing agility, rattling off Latin names in accents which betray the country of their origin. What they do not know about flowers is probably not worth knowing.

But when they are young, it is a very different matter. Consider the question of colour. If she is choosing a new colour scheme for her drawing-room the average woman is keyed up to a high pitch of excitement; indeed, she sometimes goes slightly berserk, rushing up and down the stairs with a gleam in her eyes and samples of silk rep between her teeth.

Does she carry this excitement into the garden? Does she suddenly see, in her mind's eye, a change of colour scheme that would make as thrilling a difference to an outside wall as, let us say, a change of curtains in the bedroom? She does not. She is far too inclined to leave it all to the men. Perhaps she will tell you that she is too busy about the house to have any time for these things. To some extent that is true, but not entirely. One is not asking her to go out and dig trenches, one is only asking her to use her innate taste, her natural sense of colour—in short to give her garden the same 'woman's touch' as she gives to her house.

Here is one way in which she can do it.

All over Britain, in countless suburban gardens, you will see walls covered with that fine old standby pyracantha, the firethorn, ramping up to the roof as thick as holly. The little white flowers are not impressive, but in any normal autumn the scarlet berries are superb. Indeed, at Christmas I have often used them instead of holly.

But one can grow tired of scarlet, one doesn't always want to be exactly like the woman next door. In other words, one wants a change of curtains.

So why not 'rehang' the wall with pale yellow or orange? You can do it with the same old firethorn, just as sturdy, just as swift growing, but with different berries. Like tiny lemons. And instead of the scarlet—which the Smiths and the Joneses and the Robinsons have all got—you will have this enchanting 'drape' of yellow, which is more elegant and certainly more feminine.

You will find their names in the appendix.

Now that we are talking of berries, let us consider—still with our eyes on the ladies—that old favourite the mountain ash, our native rowan. For in this tree we find another opportunity of playing new and exciting colour variations on a hackneyed theme.

Why do ninety per cent of gardeners confine themselves to the common red, whose berries are much the same as holly? If their wives were only aware that there is another variety whose berries are pale pink, surely there would be a slight domestic argument about the matter? And surely the lady would win it? A well-grown specimen of this tree is so pretty that it looks as though it were hung with costume jewellery. There is yet another sort, whose berries are of the palest yellow. If there are masculine objections—it is somewhat more expensive—the lady of the house may retort that this variety has a specially valuable quality in this day and age, when the birds are getting so rampant that sometimes we seem likely to be pecked off the face of the earth. The birds hate these yellow berries. They take one petulant bite, make a rude face, spit it out, and fly next door. Which is as it should be.

Berries are such wonderful things—little magic caskets filled with the promise of new life—that it is a pity so few of us seem to realize their possibilities. Perhaps the loveliest berry in nature is produced by a shrub that is in full bloom as I write—one of the last shrubs of summer—the *Clerodendron trichotomum*. The catalogues—such as list it—do not lie about the colour of its berries, which they describe as 'turquoise'.

When I add that these tiny jewels are set in a crimson calyx, you will have a faint idea of its beauty.

* * *

This is rather a rag-bag of a chapter; its only link is that it is primarily addressed to women.

I am assuming that all normal women like orchids. The accent is on the word 'normal' because sometimes, when mingling with the crowds who visit the orchid houses at Kew, one finds oneself standing next to women who announce in strident voices that orchids give them the creeps. '*Evil*, I call it!' they proclaim, as they stare with hostile eyes at a monstrously flamboyant *Odontoglossum* which retorts by putting out a scarlet tongue. 'It's not *healthy* . . . it's *unnatural*, that's what it is!' To give point to their words they glare in one's direction, clearly implying that any person who thinks otherwise must be addicted to nameless perversions.

I hope and believe that these ladies are exceptional and that most women share my own wonder and delight in these rich and flaming fantasies, in which Nature, quite blatantly, 'shows off'. If there is a musical analogy, as I believe there is, to all forms of beauty, then orchids must be placed in the same category as much of the music of Liszt. There is no real *reason* for those glittering cadenzas; they do not advance the argument nor illustrate the melodic theme; and presumably this is why the musical purist—who is only happy when he is listening to Bach in a howling draught at the back of the Wigmore Hall—is inclined to sneer at them, to pooh-pooh them as mere ornaments over which no serious person should waste his time. Ornaments, indeed, they are; but ornaments of such colour and brilliance, of such exquisite workmanship, that they exist, as it were, in their own emotional right. So it is with orchids; they are Nature's shameless assertion of the doctrine of art for art's sake.

How can this concern women gardeners, with small incomes, too much washing-up, and a conspicuous absence of hot-houses? Quite a lot. For they *can* grow orchids, and if their husbands do not occasionally pin bunches to their long-suffering bosoms, they have every cause for complaint. This is such a challenging statement, and may cause so much domestic argument that I will back it up by referring to my 'guarantee' to the effect that most of the flowers mentioned in my book can be inspected and 'verified' in my own modest domain.

The orchids which you can grow are called *Pleione formosana*. By the few writers who have ever referred to them, they are described as 'hardy in the open air in a sunny corner', but I rather suspect that these gentlemen live permanently in the extreme tip of Cornwall, bathed in mild sea breezes and rosy illusions. It would be safer to cultivate them, as I do, in the cold greenhouse.

What do they look like? Exactly like miniature editions of the popular mauve cattleyas which you see in fashionable florist's shops, nestling in cellophane boxes, priced at 10s. 6d. a blossom. This description may possibly put you off, because of its association with the women who so often wear them—women with large underlips, mauve lipstick and a penchant for carrying Pekinese dogs into the Savoy Grill. But please do not be deterred by these ladies; *my* orchids—I feel I have a sort of proprietary right in them—are not primarily designed for bosom-coverage, though they have looked enchanting on some, in their time. They are meant for gloating, and wonderment, and only on rare occasions for picking. They are about a third of the size of the aforesaid cattleyas, and they come in a clearer, more lambent shade of mauve.

Hardiness? Well, the only heat in my own little greenhouse comes from a small paraffin stove, which does nothing but keep out the harshest frosts. (Admittedly, we have lined it with sheets of Polythene, which is a great help.) Last year, during one of the coldest spells, the paraffin stove went out completely. There had been a rather riotous party, and one of the younger guests—always such a help about the house—went out to fill up the stove at midnight; unfortunately, instead of taking out a bottle of paraffin he equipped himself with a bottle of gin, for which the stove was not designed. On the following morning, the greenhouse had a very hang-dog look, and some of the plants that one would have thought to be comparatively hardy, such as the rose-geraniums, were killed. But the little pleiones came to no harm. After all, why should they have done, hailing as they do from the cold heights of Formosa?

PRACTICAL NOTES

I know of only two firms who supply the *Pleione formosana* orchids, though there are probably others, scattered round the country. (Details in appendix.) at the moment of writing they cost about a guinea for half a dozen. This shounds expensive, but they are very easy to divide. From a dozen plants bought a year ago I already have fifteen 'babies' which will almost certainly be in bloom in eighteen months.

How do you grow them? The orchid fiends will probably give you so much technical advice about osmunda fibre and spagnum moss that you will be put off them altogether. Forget all that. They are no more difficult than cyclamen, which means that all they want is a nice fibrous loam, to which you add peat and a little sharp sand.

However, there is one important tip to remember. Only the *base* of the bulb should be buried. Deep planting may cause them to rot. And of course, during the winter months, when the foliage has died down, you should water them very sparingly indeed—just enough to see that the soil does not cake or shrivel.

CHAPTER EIGHTEEN

A MATTER OF ARRANGEMENT

UNLESS we all blow ourselves up, the Age of Leisure
is presumably inevitable in the not too distant future,
and the thought of it has always filled me with trepi-
dation. To make an intelligent use of one's spare time
demands a high degree of culture and of application. We
all know the work that Satan finds for idle hands to do, and
some of the flower arrangements composed by ladies of
leisure at public competitions arouse a strong suspicion that
diabolic influences have already been at work.

All the same, one would have to be a churlish sort of person
to fail to welcome the popularity of this charming hobby. Of

all the minor domestic arts it is—or could be—the cheapest, the simplest and the most rewarding. One's only objection to the whole business is that the ladies who have risen to the top of the tree in the flower arrangement world—and it really is a little world of its own—are so arbitrary and dictatorial. This is particularly noticeable in America. On recent journeys through the States I have met female floral experts whose treatment of flowers recalled the conduct of a drill-sergeant in control of a squad of raw recruits. Roses, one step forward; lilies, two paces to the right; delphiniums, present arms; camellias, *charge!* I have even had the privilege of receiving personal instruction from some of these ladies. It is an intimidating experience. Armed to the teeth with pin-holders, secateurs and wire-netting they stand beside buckets of flowers delivering themselves of the sort of lecture which a general might make to his troops on the eve of an assault.

'You see, Mr Nichols, it is all a question of *balance!*' Out comes a gladiolus, dripping from the bucket, and after a moment in which she holds it at arm's length, squinting ever so slightly, she plonks it with obvious hostility into a pin-holder, not quite straight, and rather wobbly.

'Now, Mr Nichols, what does *that* suggest to you?'

It would be discourteous, in the circumstances, to reply that it merely suggests a gladiolus, not quite straight and rather wobbly. In any case, there is no time to speak.

'It suggests, does it not, a single, bold thrust of scarlet, pointing upwards? Yes. And what can *we* do with it?'

It would be even more discourteous to tell her what we can do with it, so I let her rattle on.

'We shall *marry* it—that is the word we use—we shall *marry* it to a . . . to a . . . ' (Here there is a great deal of fumbling in the bucket, in the process of which her Japanese bangles get

very wet.) 'To a red hot poker. *Kniphofia erecta*, as I am sure
I need not tell *you!*' A pause for more squinting and holding
out the kniphofia at arm's length. A sudden dart forward
and another plonk on to the pinholder. A step back. Head
on one side. A slow smile and a purring sigh. 'Yes. It is
beginning. It is *certainly* beginning! *Two* thrusts of scarlet,
pointing upwards. And where do we go from here?'

One might be pardoned for suggesting that a respectable
married woman from the neighbourhood of Ohio, after such
an emotional experience, might be well advised to retire to
her couch. But no.

The tempo is quickening. There are more frenzied dart-
ings to the water bucket, with the Japanese bangles getting
wetter and wetter. (She had been the life and soul of the
party when the local Daughters of the American Revolution
betook themselves, *en masse*, to Tokyo to learn the floral
secrets of the Japanese.) There are more inspired plonkings
into the pinholder, and the patter that accompanies these
proceedings becomes more than slightly insane.

'It is coming,' she mutters, breathing heavily. 'It is certainly coming! But it lacks movement! It needs *sweep* . . .
and we can give it, yes, no, *yes* . . . we can give it sweep with
this bee-yeau-tiful beetroot leaf! (Out it comes, and it is
indeed a beautiful leaf, ribbed with scarlet, but she sticks it
in at such a violent angle that it makes the whole arrangement look like a picture hat blown sideways in a gale.)
'There is our sweep! There is our height! There is our balance! But something is lacking. Light! We must have light!'
And into the bucket she dives for light, which emerges in the
shape of three rather battered white cornflowers. And I
really cannot go on like this. But I can assure you that the
flower arrangement queens really do go on like this, and that

the portrait is not exaggerated.

All of which seems to be rather a pity, for these antics turn what should be an amiable diversion into a tense and exacting chore, attended by a great deal of nervous strain.

Arranging flowers for the sheer fun of it—wandering round a garden with a basket and a pair of scissors on a summer evening must surely be one of the most therapeutic occupations ever devised, and it is not surprising to learn that courses in flower arrangement are regularly prescribed by American psychiatrists in the treatment of certain female neuroses. But unless the flower arrangers loosen up, they will soon be creating these neuroses instead of curing them.

This reminds me of a rather macabre incident that occurred during a recent visit to America. I had been lecturing in one of those small towns, not a thousand miles from New England, where life seems to have stood still for a couple of centuries. (Only in America can an Englishman step back into the eighteenth century without finding anything to offend him. In Newport, Rhode Island, for example, one has the feeling that one could walk gaily down the High Street, in knee-breeches and a powdered wig, inhaling snuff and twirling a cane, without causing any comment.) After the lecture I promised to stay on to judge the flower arrangement competition which was to be held on the following day, and since the flowers were already set in their appointed niches I asked permission to go down and look at them by myself in the evening, without any distracting influences. So they gave me a key, and after dinner I set out to the little local hall, opened the door, and switched on the porch light. For a moment I stared into the semi-darkness, which glowed with the colours of the rainbow from the bunches ranged round the walls. I was about to switch on the top lights when

I realized that I was not alone. At the far end of the hall was a small female who, even in the shadows, suggested that she was not quite 'all there'; her hat was tilted at a rakish angle and her long scarf trailed over her shoulders into the dust. Apart from this, she was softly humming the Jewel Song from *Faust*, in a cracked soprano, which, you must admit, was an odd thing to do in the circumstance. As she hummed, shuffling slowly past the exhibits, she projected a small claw-like hand, tugged a blossom from the arrangement opposite her, and shuffled on. It was most disturbing. '*Oh! Je ris . . .*' she croaked, '*de me voir si belle—dans ce miroir!*' With each phrase the claw came out, and a carnation dropped on to the floor, or a peony or a rose, and some woman's floral dream-child was shattered. This was definitely one of those situations in which I did not wish to be involved, so I tiptoed away. If this were a fictional story one could invent a dramatic scene for the following morning, and lay a lot of cunning clues pointing to the suspect. But there was no dramatic scene, though some of the ladies, admittedly, looked rather hot and bothered, and most of the bunches had a faintly dishevelled appearance.

This small episode might well be an example of our suggestion that the art of flower arrangement, when carried to extremes, can produce those neuroses it is intended to cure. For though it would be absurd to say that it has led to the break-up of homes, it has certainly been responsible for a great deal of female acrimony, particularly in the American Garden Clubs. And this, as I said, is due to the dictatorial methods of the ladies who lay down the law, the lecturers and writers who make up the rules.

For really, there *are* no rules. Either you can do it, or you can't. It is as simple as that. Like making music. Given, say, five notes—E, F sharp, G natural, B natural and B sharp (I am writing away from a piano but that does not affect the argument)—the mind of the music-maker automatically shapes these notes into a melodic phrase whose character is determined by the rhythm in which he happens to be thinking. In the same way, given a handful of flowers and grasses, the eyes of a born artist automatically sets them in a pattern that sings. She does *not* natter on about 'balance' or 'sweep' or 'weight' or 'light'.

And yet, though this is not an art that can be taught, it is something which improves with practice. And since I have had rather more than my share of practice, let us try to be practical about it in the chapter that follows.

Miscanthus
sinensis

Pampas grass

CHAPTER NINETEEN

A MIXED BUNCH

W E are going to share the great delight of arranging a
mixed bunch of flowers, so let us begin by considering
the ingredients with which we have to work—not only
the flowers themselves, but the leaves and the foliage, which
may be even more important.

Here are a few rather out-of-the-way suggestions that
might—I only say might—be useful, if you are toying with the
idea of entering for next year's flower competition. What
you do with them is your own affair. It may result in a botch
or it may result in a masterpiece. But at least you will have a
rather wider choice than the lady next door.

So begin with the foliage. And in particular with the leaves of that very same beetroot which our American friend used in her bunch. It is called Ruby Chard, and even if you never bother to eat the vegetable itself—though it is delicious and, so they tell me, rich in iron—the leaves are so beautiful that you will want to grow the plant for these alone. The stems and veins are of an eye-catching red, like vermilion sealing wax. I would not be so impertinent as to suggest how you might use these leaves, but you might care to think of them as a sort of rich, solid base on which to pile up other improvization in the theme of red.

After the beet come the hostas. I have already written of these, so we need not go on about them, apart from emphasizing, once more, their unique qualities of colour when they fade with the fading year.

Now for ornamental grasses. These, I hope you will agree, can be sheer hell. A well-grown 'pampas grass', sited in the middle of a suburban lawn, with all those ghastly feather dusters sticking out of it, can be as embarrassing as a middle-aged lady standing on the steps of a provincial town hall, disguised as Cleopatra after the annual fancy dress ball at the Rotary Club. But there are other grasses of the greatest elegance, which I have never seen used by anybody but myself, and of these I would give pride of place to zebra grass (*Miscanthus sinensis zebrinus*). If you were to see this growing by the side of my small pond, where it reaches a height of five feet, you would realize how aptly it is named, for the leaves, long and arching, are dappled with stripes of pale gold. Even on a dull day, if you let your eyes wander through the foliage, you have the impression of a little wood in which the sunlight is filtering through the branches. In full sunshine, when the leaves are reflected in the water, it is a brilliant, dancing thing. It grows so quickly and abundantly that you can cut substantial branches of it without making any noticeable difference to the bush. And though it might be rash to say that an arranger could not go wrong with it—for some people could make even an egg-cupful of dog violets look *outré*—it is really difficult to see how anybody could make a hash of this. It 'arranges' itself.

The zebra grass is best suited for lofty and majestic occasions. For more modest decorations, I would recommend another grass, which must surely be among the most delightful conceits ever devised by Nature. (Sometimes I wonder if in fact it was not designed by Walt Disney.) This small charmer is afflicted with the name of *Pennisetum villosum*. Why it should be so burdened is a mystery, for when it is in seed it produces feathery nonsenses which suggest the tails of very small and ethereal rabbits bouncing in and out of a Disney playground. In case this description strikes you as faintly arch, which is all too likely, here is a more sober account. Height, eighteen inches. Habit, arching. Seed-pods very feathery, ivory white, sometimes tinged with mauve. Usually classed as an annual, but seeds itself so freely that it can be regarded as a perennial.

Now that I have mentioned the rabbits' tails produced by this grass, I shall take leave to boast of one of my own small inventions in this charming game. This is called the Dandelion Clock design. I live in a very dandeliony district and toward the end of June the air is thick with their delicate, but very troublesome seeds. One day I wondered if it might not be possible to put the seed clusters to a useful purpose, so I gathered a bunch, picking them one by one, and transporting them very gingerly indoors, with one hand protecting them from the wind. Then I set them in a pinholder, and gradually introduced among them a rustic company of field grasses and buttercups and wild daisies. After which I set them under a Victorian case, to save them from draughts and the possible assaults of pussies. This is a slow business, you need most of the morning for it; you also need a very steady hand. But I cannot conceive a morning more agreeably spent, and the clocks and the flowers, even the buttercups, last much longer than you would imagine—for nearly a week if you are lucky.

Are you troubled with moles? Not moles on the chin, but moles in the ground. This abrupt question is posed with the object of drawing your attention to the caper spurge, *Euphorbia lathyrus*, a bold and handsome plant which also comes into the class that we grow for foliage. A single sniff of it, apparently, is enough to fill the moles with profound depression and send them off in search of other quarters. Moles or no moles the species called Snow on the Mountain, *Euphorbia marginata*, is very beautiful indeed, and well worthy of its name; the upper leaves are snow white, gradually tinged with green as you look down the stem. It is so compact and delicate that it is sometimes worn as a buttonhole. This might give you some ideas for using it in a Victorian posy.

*   *   *

And now I have already written enough to break my own rule that flower arrangement is something that cannot be taught. So I will not offer any more suggestions as to the type of flowers you might use. They have probably all been written about before.

But some tricks of this engaging trade have *not* been written about, at any rate, to my knowledge. Such as the use of mirrors. Very few seem to have grasped the possibilities of the common looking-glass. This seems very odd, if only for economic reasons; after all, six roses in front of a mirror automatically become a dozen roses. But there is more to it than that; it is not only a matter of money and mathematics; the six roses are not merely duplicated but given, as it were, an extra dimension. Magic gets to work—the same magic that held sway in the world of Alice. Moreover, with a mirror you can play tricks of light and shade that would otherwise be impossible, and if the mirror is a beautiful one, you have, ready made, a frame for your composition which will give it an added dignity and importance. In my own not very grandiose music-room, as I have almost certainly boasted before, there is a very beautiful Chippendale mirror, which was hung in its present position for the sole purpose of reflecting flowers. Below it is a gilt console table on which stands a gilt Regency wine-cooler, always waiting to be filled. The whole room centres round this trio—the mirror, the table, and the vase; it is a little golden stage on which we can display the changing pageant of the year. Even bare branches look beautiful in it, and after them come the green waterfalls of the catkins, and after that the drama gains sparkle and brilliance, week by week. The secret of the success of dramas is the permanence of their setting. That small stage was not created without a great deal of thought and experiment. Even if I were back in my bedsitting room days, I should begin by creating such a setting, though it might only be an earthenware jug in a niche of the bookcase, so long as the flowers were in a position to catch the light where it would most flatter them.

And that reminds me, very few flower arrangers pay enough attention to lighting, which is as important in the drawing-room as on the stage. They shove flowers into dark corners, or into places where only half of a bunch catches the sun, or—worst of all—directly under a brilliant top light which robs them of all their delicacy of colour. At the risk of sounding as though I were claiming to be exceptionally sensitive, I really feel, at times, that some people literally do not see what is there to be seen, just as some people do not hear what is there to be heard. (How, otherwise, can one account for the fact that many people will sit talking, quite happily, to the accompaniment of sounds from the radio which, to some of us, are like sharp poisoned swords, slashing pitilessly and remorsely at our ear-drums?)

Try a simple experiment. Arrange a bunch, say of freesias —not that they need much 'arranging'; set them in a slender glass vase, and place them on a table by the window in full sunlight. Move them a foot to the right, a foot to the left, a foot to the rear. Take them out of the light and put them in semi-shade. If you study them carefully, while you are doing this, you will notice that with each move the picture becomes totally different. At one moment they might be flowers de-signed to lie on the bosom of a maiden by Marie Laurencin, pale and pastel and indeterminate, at the next they are as clear-cut and incisive as an eighteenth-century print. And then they suddenly turn into a Fantin-Latour.

*　　*　　*

One bunch of my own I shall always remember, if only because the making of it nearly cost me my life.

A number of us were asked to arrange flowers to be exhibited for charity at the Royal Horticultural Hall. Cecil Beaton, they said, was going to do something quite staggering, in the intervals between designing the dresses for *My Fair Lady*. Oliver Messel was taking time off from devising the scenery for a new production of *The Magic Flute* at Covent Garden. Norman Hartnell was shaking from his hair the thousands of sequins which were being sewn on to the dress which the Queen had chosen for the official dinner with the President of France. Constance Spry, it was rumoured, would descend on us—and, I suspected, outshine us all—with a positive cornucopia of flowers, and fruit. There was even a hope that Picasso might be induced to fly over and do something very important with a trio of vegetable marrows sliced in half and stuffed with artificial moustaches. (To be entitled 'The Three Virgins of Valencia'.) This hope, odd as it may seem, I did not share.

Faced by such competition, one would obviously have to take rather more than the usual amount of trouble, so I went out into the garden to think. I was quite determined that all the flowers should come from my own garden; other people might have recourse to flower shops, not me. (Even a single 'shop' carnation in a country bunch seems to put the whole thing out of focus, like a woman in a Dior dress at a meeting of the parish council.) Very soon the design began to take shape. The south wall of the cottage was a mass of deep red Etoile de Hollande roses, just coming into bud. There was a lovely cluster of Sweet Williams, the colour of tawny port. In the cold greenhouse there were several pots of achingly scarlet geraniums—Beatrix Little variety. There were a number of superb cherry-red peonies which would clash excitingly with the crimson phloxes. By the time I had finished my tour I had selected all the reds that you will find in Roget's *Thesaurus*: lobster, post-office, sealing-wax, lake, cherry, cochineal—the lot. It would be a positive orgy of red, and

Cecil and Oliver and Norman and all the rest would be put to shame by it. Particularly when it was set in the old Regency wine-cooler and backed by a single dramatic sweep of copper beech.

This was three days before the great event.

And then, on the following morning, the weather suddenly decided to misbehave. The temperature dropped precipitously, and a wind straight from Siberia swept across the lawn, causing the buds of the roses on which the whole design was based to close up in disgust. There was nothing to do but to cut them and bring them into the tool-shed. But even there, the conditions were so glacial that they stubbornly refused to open. They needed at least twenty-four hours of real heat.

So on the following day I took them up to London—together with all the other reds—set them in front of the fire in the little Chelsea flat—turned on the gas, and went out to lunch. I came back to look at them at tea time; they were beginning to respond, and I encouraged them by prising open some of the petals. Then I went out to a cocktail party, firmly determined to sit up with them, if necessary, all night, in a tropical heat.

It must have been a very good cocktail party. For when I came back all I remember after putting two more shillings in the meter, is an indeterminate haze of red, a slow opening of buds, a swift closing of eyelids, and some hours later, an agonized choking and a hideous smell. Something, as you will have guessed, had gone wrong with the gas. The final scene of the drama was enacted on the steps in the street outside, where I had managed to crawl, to an audience of a not very sympathetic policeman.

All the same, it was worth it. My little bunch—no, really,

that is hardly the word for it, since it dwarfed all the others
by its sheer bulk—won its award. Not only from the President
of the Royal Horticultural Society but—even more important
—from Constance Spry herself, the greatest of them all.

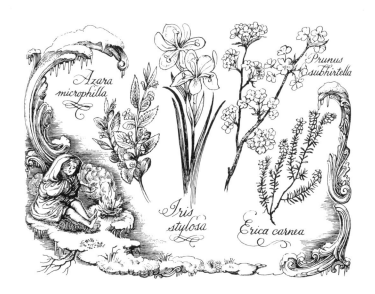

Azara
microphilla

Iris
stylosa

Prunus
subhirtella

Erica carnea

CHAPTER TWENTY

WINTER GLORY

A PSYCHIATRIST once hinted that my special love of winter flowers was a complex—a sort of regrettable Peter Panism, which caused its victims subconsciously to reject the inevitable natural sequence of growth, decay and death.

If, by this, he meant that I refused to admit that there was ever a time of the year when the garden need cease to bloom, that there was not a single day, even in the snow, when it must be shrouded in dust sheets, then he was perfectly right. The best gardeners are three-hundred-and-sixty-five-day-a-year gardeners, for long experience has taught them that some of the darkest days can also be among the brightest.

On my desk, as I write on this bleak December day, is a vase of pale blue *Iris unquicularis*—previously known as 'stylosa'—which of all winter flowers I would put the first. I have praised this flower before but I make no apologies for praising it again, and I shall probably go on doing so until people start planting it in sheer self defence.

For, just look at this vase! The flowers are as lovely as any orchid, the colour of the sky on a clear day in early March, faintly flecked with gold. They are so frail and delicate that if you bend over them they tremble to your breath. And yet, only twelve hours ago they were buried two feet deep under a snow drift. They were picked, of course, in bud and brought indoors to open. In a warm room they open so quickly that you can sit and watch them do it.

Sometimes—indeed more often than not—people baffle me. They drive through roaring gales to come to dinner, they stamp the snow off their boots in the porch, they rush to the fire to warm their sit-upons, and then they look round the room, observe the bowls of gleaming *Iris unquicularis*, and gasp. (I need hardly say that such people would not be seasoned gardeners; *they* would merely observe acidly that it had been such an exceptional year for irises that one hardly knew what to do with them, did one?) But the others really do gasp, and begin at once to talk in italics. *What* are they? *Where* did I get them? Out of a *hot-house* of course? *No?* But then . . . *I* must have green fingers! To which I feel like retorting: 'Green fingers, my foot.' It has nothing to do with green fingers. All that is needed is a sunny wall and good drainage, plus a barrow-full of gravel round the roots. And I nearly forgot—eighteen shillings to pay for half a dozen clumps. You do not have to be a Rothschild to grow these irises, but you will feel very like a Rothschild after doing so. They are so tough and so accommodating that if you do not succeed with them there must be something radically wrong with your heart or your hands or your head, or all three. Unless, of course, there is something horrible lurking in the wood-shed, which creeps out to attack them in the night.

* * *

Of most of the standard mid-winter flowers, as I said above, I have written before, but in the past few years I have made a few discoveries which may be unfamiliar to the average gardener. The first of these—*Azara microphylla*—is rewarding for an unusual reason, because of its scent. It smells so strongly of vanilla that on sunny days, when little boys walk past the railings of my cottage, they pause and their noses twitch, as though they were saying to themselves: 'The ice-cream man cometh.'

The azara has tiny leaves, deep green and glossy, growing on drooping stems. It also has tiny flowers, white and very modest. Since it is not too easy to transplant, it will probably produce only two or three of these flowers in the first season, so that if you hover round it, hoping for a delicious sensuous experience in a January blizzard, nothing will happen at all, except that you will end up by catching cold and cursing the author of these words.

But if you will only have patience, and wait till the second year, you *will* have the aforesaid 'delicious sensuous experience'. Not in a January blizzard, but in the transitory moments when winter smiles and the sun comes out and the coats come off. There is something almost perversely stimulating in its strange South Seas perfume, drifting up through the sharp crisp air, mingling with the wood-smoke from the bonfire over the way.

PRACTICAL NOTE

The azara is not tough nor is it unduly tender. I know of several specimens that have withstood the most inhospitable conditions in these islands—in the bleak Midlands, on the coast of Northumberland, even on the heights of Hampstead. The one essential is a wall—if possible, in a corner formed by two walls, because it is a wind-hater.

*　　*　　*

We began this chapter with a bunch of irises. There is another little vase, over there on the piano, filled with winter flowers. Let us go and look at it.

In this there are all old winter favourites to which I have been faithful ever since the days of *Down the Garden Path*, when on a bleak December afternoon I had the first, and maybe the greatest, thrill of my whole gardening career—the sight of the rosy spikes of winter heather thrusting through the snow. That was one of those moments in life when one felt that God had indeed been a loving Father, sending the flowers with the snow, and giving one eyes to see them, and fingers to touch them, as one bent down and very gently flicked away the snow from the petals. The afternoon was unearthly quiet, and I can still hear the ghostly tinkle of those heather bells across the years, and the soft sigh of the snow as it fell to earth.

But we must try to be practical. In the many seasons which have lapsed since that December afternoon the winter heathers have gained in strength and deepened in colour. Of all the newer varieties none is sturdier nor more glowing than *Erica carnea*, Eileen Porter. This flowers from November till March, and is unblemished by the sharpest frost. Of the whites the *Erica carnea*, Springwood White, is still unbeaten. A bank of this precious thing when the snow is around is something to live for—white against white, each trying to outshine the other.

PRACTICAL NOTE

Both these winter heathers, indeed, all the carneas, tolerate lime, which alas is not the case with the summer varieties. As they are creatures of the moorland it would seem hardly necessary to say that they like an open position. You can buy good plants for about 3s. and increase them either by cuttings or by layering. The Springwood White is a lovely 'layerer'; it sends out small green arms at the end of which are little hands that clutch down into the earth as though they were determined to cling to life while they had the chance.

*　　*　　*

Back to our vase. You have to have a touch of the 'shrinker' about you to share my love of these winter delights; some of them are so small that they might have been designed to decorate a doll's house. Which reminds me that perhaps the most endearing example of flower decoration I ever saw was contained in a doll's house. It dated from Queen Anne, and stood about four feet high, like a three-tiered corner cupboard. The old lady who owned it had furnished the floors in three different periods. The ground floor was a Georgian dining-room with the prettiest set of Sheraton chairs, the middle floor was Regency with a striped wallpaper, and a grand gilt candelabrum, the top floor was early Victorian, with horsehair sofas and a grand piano, the size of one's thumb, draped in a Scottish tartan. In each of these rooms were mixed bunches of miniature flowers and grasses and leaves, most cunningly contrived, with all the things that 'shrinkers' love. One particularly effective bunch was composed of seeding grass against a background of pine-needles. People who like their delphiniums to grow to the height of guardsmen would have thought very little of it.

They might think equally little of the bunch on my piano. For example, they might scarcely notice the spray of winter cherry, *Prunus subhirtella autumnalis,* in the centre, but I should like you to notice it, for if any winter flowering tree is fool-proof, this is it. By fool-proof I do not mean that you can expect it to flourish in a slag-heap or on a storm-tossed island off the north coast of Scotland, but it will stand any amount of wind and though a very sharp frost will turn the petals brown, they flower again and again, and in any normal winter you will have blossom from November to the end of February.

Today, this prunus affords yet another example of the skill of our nurserymen. Thirty years ago the variety *rosea* was in very short supply and cost at least five guineas for a rather weedy specimen. But now you can buy sturdy five-foot trees all over the country for 17s. 6d. I recommend this variety rather than the ordinary *autumnalis* because the petals are flushed with pale pink. And a gleam of pale pink outside the window, on a grey December morning, makes Surrey much easier to put up with when one's friends send one postcards from Jamaica.

CHAPTER TWENTY-ONE

'GARDEN OPEN TODAY'

THE discerning reader will very quickly discover that this chapter has nothing to teach him about how to deal with black-fly on the broad beans. But sometimes in a book, as in a garden, the author feels that he has earned the right to relax—and so, no doubt, does the reader! In the past few chapters there have been quite a number of difficult flower names to remember. And since we have promised to produce these flowers on request, a-growing and a-blowing, this might be a fitting moment to study from behind the scenes some of the many dilemmas and comedies which the owner of a garden will encounter when he unlocks his garden gate and admits the outside world.

As far as we were concerned, when we welcomed our first

batch of visitors, three years after the garden was born, the most pressing problem was presented by the cats. What was to be done about them? 'Four' and 'Five' would certainly go stark staring mad if they were suddenly to meet hordes of strangers walking down their private, personal paths; the weekly visit of the dustmen—a comparatively undramatic event, to which one would have thought they would by now have accustomed themselves—invariably induced a nervous crisis, impelling them to dart in terror across the lawn, as though pursued by fiends. On the other hand, Oscar would go equally stark and staring if he were shut up. The least restriction on Oscar's liberty is the immediate signal for piteous wails and frenzied scratchings on doors. Besides, Oscar is naturally gregarious; he is a pushover for people. The word 'pushover' is to be literally interpreted; it means that when friends come to call, and when we are having tea on the lawn, Oscar arrives, making polite conversation, and stands there waiting to be pushed on to his back, in order that he may lie on the grass with his paws dangling at a suitably alluring angle, regarding us through his green, Chinese eyes.

However—and this was the root of the matter—Oscar, being a not very well cat, was exceptionally thin, whereas 'Four' and 'Five' were exceptionally plump. How was this to be explained to the large numbers of cat lovers whom we were confidently expecting? This was indeed a dark and difficult situation. 'Four' and 'Five' would be locked up in the study—immense, glossy creatures, bursting with vitamins, a superb advertisement for their master, but nobody would see them. Meanwhile Oscar would be stalking here there and everywhere, greatly enjoying himself, but so gaunt and spectral, so obviously undernourished, with his ribs sticking through his fur, that the public would be justified in thinking that we fed him on water and stale crusts.

What was to be done? I could not spend the entire after-noon explaining that Oscar's daily diet included milk, a large whiting, elevenses, part of my lunch, another whiting, at least one tin of cat food, more milk, and various tit-bits of rabbit, beef and chicken. If 'Four' and 'Five' had eaten half as much, they would have been extremely sick. But in Oscar's case, the food simply went straight through him, and he looked, and I am afraid will always look, like the alley cat to end all alley cats. Which is perhaps why I love him so much.

What would *you* have done? What we did was I think ingenious. We persuaded 'Four' and 'Five' to make brief appearances at the window, rather like extremely plump prima donnas taking curtain calls, and they were so vast and glistening, so obviously replenished with the good things of the earth, that they allayed to some extent the unfortunate impression created by Oscar's emaciation. True, a few suspicious characters hinted that 'Four' and 'Five' must be pampered favourites, while Oscar was a sort of feline Cin-derella, but these unkind people were in the minority.

The cats were also the indirect means of illustrating a simple little garden gadget which I have not seen elsewhere. And though the circumstances were somewhat embarras-sing, the device has proved so useful that I will briefly explain it.

Like many people whose gardens adjoin the estates of others, large and small, I am honoured by the visits of neigh-bouring felines. They appear dramatically on the tops of walls, spying out the land (all cats, of course, are in the secret service), or they dart from out of the darkness of the tool-shed. Sometimes they stroll, with apparent nonchalance, across the open lawn, which gives rise to scenes of great tension if any of my own cats happen to be engaged in counter-espionage at the windows, as they often are. Generally speaking, we are in the usual state of armed neutrality, which is common to the cat world; it is only seldom that the cold war explodes into a hot one, with all the dreadful siren wails of feline onslaught, and the sharp deadly 'hick' which always brings to mind the release of poison gas.

There is only one drawback to these visitors, or rather, to one of them. At certain times of the year, a certain uninhibited tom-cat—I am naming no names—decides that certain of my small trees were specially planted for a certain purpose, which may be roughly described as powdering the nose. And round the garden he parades, on spring evenings, powdering his nose with such persistence that the poor little trees, mostly miniature cypresses, go brown and eventually die. Now if this particular tom-cat were a character in a play by Mr Tennessee Williams such conduct would naturally be regarded as entirely *comme il faut*, and would probably gain him an Oscar. But in my small domain it was frowned upon.

So what did we do? We bought a quantity of Polythene and draped it gracefully round the base of the trees in order that the tom-cat could go on powdering its nose without doing any harm. I am aware that this solution can be attacked from two angles. The Tennessee Williams' school might protest that by so doing we were running the risk of giving the tom-cat complexes, and ruining its chances of a full emotional life; the anti-cat school would observe tersely, that it would be simpler to reach for a brick. As you may have observed we belong to neither of these schools, so we used the Polythene.

Unfortunately, when the garden was opened I forgot to

remove the Polythene, which immediately attracted the amiable attention of large numbers of elderly ladies. 'What a charming idea!' they crooned. 'What is it for? Is it to keep the dear little trees warm round the bottom?' If anybody can think of a suitable riposte to that question I shall be much obliged.

*   *   *

Even without these complications, opening one's garden is an event that is attended by a certain amount of drama—the sort of quiet domestic drama in which the tension gradually rises, and reaches a climax on the eve of the great day, when the posters are nailed to the garden gate. Gaskin always charges himself with this task, and emerges on to the common armed with a handful of drawing-pins, and a sheaf of placards and streamers which, if the affair is in the cause of charity, have been kindly sent down from London. He nails one to the garden gate, one to the railings and one to the giant sycamore outside the front door, after which he disposes the streamers at strategic positions on various trees along the road. These activities usually engage the attention of a number of small boys, who gather round him with a faintly menacing aspect. They also attract a number of stray dogs, who sniff around the tree trunks, gaze up at the streamers and depart, having expressed their opinion in the classical canine manner.

Meanwhile, I am watching the proceedings through a chink in the curtains, feeling not unlike the proprietor of a tea-shop. If one is not used to being 'in business', there is a curious sense of nudity when you invite the public inside the doors of your establishment, even if the cause is a worthy one, and I often wonder if this sensation is shared by shopkeepers when they first see their names in bold letters on a busy street. Certainly, when I see people gathering round the posters I feel like rushing out and saying to them: 'There is certainly no *need* to come in . . . it is only a suggestion.' And if they look rather shabby and dirty I also feel like telling them that they can come in free. Indeed I once did this very thing, with disastrous results, in the case of a very depressed looking couple who were accompanied by two hoydenish little boys who looked as if they had not had a bath for a week. They were gazing wistfully through the gate into the garden, and in a moment of expansion I went up to them and said please would they walk inside and not bother about the entrance fee because I could see how things were with them. They glared at me with an outraged expression and then, without a word, turned briskly about and stalked back to their Rolls. It afterwards transpired that they were a family of millionaires, who had sent their children to one of those advanced schools in which the curriculum includes a brisk course in elementary arson.

This pre-opening atmosphere of tension is heightened by the behaviour of the garden itself; quite invariably everything is either too backward or too forward, and one has visions of oneself spending the afternoon doing a super Ruth Draper act . . . 'If only you had come last week!' 'If only you could see it in a fortnight!' There is a terrible temptation to rush into the market, at the last moment, and buy quantities of pot plants in full bloom, to fill in the blank spaces. This temptation, up till now, I have resisted, not for any lofty moral reason but because such chicanery would almost certainly be detected. For always, among the visitors, is a sprinkling of experts—gnarled old ladies who bombard one with terrifying questions about species of rhododendrons or gentle, soft-spoken middle-aged men, disguised as chartered accountants, who suddenly disclose themselves as the authors of a standard work on auriculas.

How shall one answer them? What will one do to avoid exposure? The air is thick with questions. Supposing it doesn't rain, and everybody comes, and there is a traffic jam? Supposing a gigantic policeman snorts up on a motor-bicycle and tells one to stop it?

Supposing we are visited by the gossip writer from the *Daily Blank*—one of those sweet young creatures born with a mini-camera built into the bosom—and supposing she darts off to the telephone booth and earns a brisk fifteen guineas with a front page story: 'Author Stops Traffic'?

But perhaps the most urgent question is: 'Shall we keep people to the garden or shall we let them into the house as well?' My first reaction was to keep them to the garden, for the simple reason that I did not feel justified in asking people to waste their time examining my very modest bits and pieces. For a few shillings they could wander through galleries of masterpieces at Blenheim and such places, whereas what had I to show? Only a few pretty chairs . . . and my Richard Wilson screen . . . and the Canaletto . . . ('school of !'). But the Chinese Chippendale mirror was worth looking at and the Regency suite in the dining-room . . . well maybe it was not so bad. And I could display, very prominently, my solitary snob photograph which Mr Somerset Maugham had sent me one Christmas, showing him sitting by the side of Sir Winston Churchill on the terrace of the Villa Mauresque. I can never look at it without remembering Noël Coward's enchanting remark about Mr Maugham's striking cast of countenance: 'Dear Willie Maugham—the original Lizard of Oz.'

Anyway, in the end, we decided to let people inside. I have never regretted it and the experience, each year, has been increasingly happy. After nearly a thousand people—many of them in very modest circumstances—had trooped through my tiny rooms there was less to clear up than after a small cocktail party. Perhaps the attitude of the average visitor was summed up by a very pretty girl who works in a neighbouring factory. As soon as she had walked through the garden gate she stared at the lawn, which admittedly was looking very nice, and then she stared at her shoes, and then she said: 'Not in these heels!' Whereupon she went home on her motor bike and returned half an hour later wearing sandals. In this day and age, which is hardly characterized by any general respect for other people's property, such a gesture is refreshing, to say the least of it.

Well, we have had our moment of relaxation. It is time to turn the page and tackle the final section—the appendix. In spite of the unalluring title I hope you will read it, because it will help to bring within your actual grasp the whole range of flowers and trees and shrubs which we have discussed in the foregoing chapters.

APPENDIX

This is very much a one-man appendix, in the sense that the nurserymen, seedsmen and horticultural suppliers mentioned in it are, with very few exceptions, people with whom I have had personal dealings. Obviously this must limit its scope; no single gardener, even if he lived to be a hundred, could have personal experience of all the nurserymen scattered over the British Isles. However, if this section is to have any value it must be a personal one. It would have been easy to compile long lists of firms merely on the strength of their reputations, but such a list would not have been of much practical use. Besides, the firms with the greatest reputations are not always the firms with the best goods. For example, there is one very famous firm of seedsmen whose very name makes me see red. Every time I pass their glittering exhibit at the Chelsea Flower Show I feel like leaping over the railings and delivering a speech to the assembled multitudes, warning them that nothing they buy from Messrs X's will ever 'come up'.

You will not find the name of Messrs X's in the following pages.

Before we get down to brass tacks I must emphasize, at the outset *the paramount importance to every gardener of equipping himself with an adequate collection of commercial catalogues*. If this appendix served no other purpose than to bring these catalogues to your attention it would still be worth reading.

Were I beginning a gardening career on a limited income, and were I offered a choice between £10 worth of books on 'how to garden' and a collection of nurserymen's catalogues at half a crown apiece, post free, I would unhesitatingly choose the catalogues. Apart from the fact that they are usually written in better English, they have a direct, down-to-earth quality which brings their wares into sharp relief. These men write of what they know, and because they are writing, as it were, with a price-tag attached to their pens, they stick to facts.

Moreover, they contain a vast amount of practical information. What to plant, how to plant, when to plant, where to plant.

There are a number of 'classic' catalogues of British nurserymen, without which no gardening library can be regarded as complete. I have most of them, and a great deal they have taught me, but we must use our space only for those few with whom I have had personal dealings.

Let us begin with:

TREES AND SHRUBS

Here, in alphabetical order, are some of the catalogues which can be described as 'musts'.

> The Nurseries,
> Hillier & Sons Ltd,
> Winchester.

The most comprehensive, informative and authoritative of all catalogues on trees and shrubs.

> George Jackman & Sons,
> Woking Nurseries Ltd,
> Woking, Surrey.

Particularly good for clematis, cherries and other fruit trees, crabs and acers, dwarf conifers ... but read it for yourself. Incidentally, the pages of this catalogue offer some of the best prose now being written in the English language. Clean, strong, and delicate. Somebody at Jackman's seems to have missed his vocation. I hope he continues to miss it.

> L. R. Russell Ltd,
> Richmond Nurseries,
> Windlesham,
> Surrey.

Here you are welcomed like a duke even if you have only come to buy a few yards of privet.

> John Scott & Co.,
> Merriott,
> Somerset.

Theirs is a very beautiful catalogue, lavishly illustrated with woodcuts which oddly enough, really look like the plants they celebrate.

And three others:

> Sunningdale Nurseries,
> Windlesham,
> Surrey.

> John Waterer Sons & Crisp Ltd,
> The Floral Mile,
> Twyford,
> Berkshire.

> R. C. Notcutt Ltd,
> Woodbridge,
> Suffolk.

I have certainly omitted the names of many distinguished

and honourable firms. As I have observed before, only too often, one can only write of what one knows.

These catalogues are vital. With them the beginner enters realms of delight through which, if he is lucky, he will wander for the rest of his life.

*　　*　　*

In a moment, we shall be bringing forward a number of nurserymen, some of them comparatively obscure, to make their bow before us, catalogues in hand.

But first, since we have begun by mentioning trees and shrubs, let us emphasize another point of importance. *The nurseryman cannot do all the work.* He can raise your plants, he can tend them for years, watering them, staking and pruning them, keeping them free from disease, and when the time comes he can lift them and deliver them to your front door. Here his responsibility ends and yours begins. It is such a heavy responsibility that I am going to look forward for a moment, assuming that you have actually written for your catalogues, and chosen your trees, and that the great day has arrived when a lorry drives up with a bundle addressed to you—a living bundle—in which there is sleeping a small world of beauty. Are you ready for it? Are you in the right *mental* condition to take charge of it?

Look at it like this.

Imagine that you were:

(*a*) Subjected to a severe surgical operation.

(*b*) Tightly strapped in coarse straw bandages.

(*c*) Compelled, immediately afterwards, to take a long railway journey standing up in the guard's van, sometimes for several days, deprived of food or water.

It is conceivable, in these circumstances, that at the end

of your journey you might feel in need of a little moral and physical support. But if you were a tree or a flowering shrub the odds are that you would not get it.

I have been planting trees all my life—every sort of tree and shrub from forest conifers to miniature azaleas, in every variety of soil and weather. And the reason I have had scarcely one per cent of casualties is because I have always regarded a tree, when it arrives, as a hospital case, to be given immediate and expert attention. Try to do the same. And try *not* to do the following:

1. Do *not* dig your holes in advance, particularly if you live in a heavy soil, in the mistaken idea that you will be able to pop the tree in with a minimum of delay. Wait till it arrives. If you dig a hole in advance, ten to one it will start to pour with rain, and you will be faced with a repulsive puddle of congealed mud with which the delicate roots cannot possibly cope.

By all means prepare the soil, forking it to a depth of two feet to lighten it and to get rid of weeds and surface roots. And have a nice little pile of peat handy to dig in. Leave it at that.

2. Don't try to plant it all by yourself. If it is true that it takes God to make a tree, it is equally true that it takes two humans to plant it—unless it is very small and unless you are a very old hand at the game. You want somebody to hold it straight, and most important of all, to jiggle it.

By 'jiggling' I mean agitating the trunk gently but firmly up and down so that the loose soil is shaken all round the fibrous roots. Many trees have roots shaped like claws, and if you just pile the earth on top of them you leave empty gaps underneath.

3. Don't skimp your staking, for staking is the most vital part of all. Wind, as we have seen, is the gardener's greatest enemy. After all, your tree is a convalescent, it has had a

nasty shock, and if it is constantly wind-rocked during the coming winter it may never recover.

One elemental but often forgotten rule is to drive in your stake *before* you shovel in the soil. If you wait till the soil has been put back, you can't see what you are doing, and you may be driving the stake right through a delicate root.

Planting a tree is one of the most satisfying things a man can do. When you plant a tree you are perpetuating life, enriching the lovely land you live in, storing up a treasure house of beauty for your old age. Please plant it properly.

*   *   *

Now the nurserymen can take the stage:
Let us begin with:

FLOWER SEEDS

It was Mr Page, my gardening guide, friend and counsellor, who first introduced me to those great seed merchants:

> Messrs Thompson & Morgan,
> The Nurseries,
> Ipswich.

How this establishment, with its world-wide connections, had previously evaded me, I cannot imagine. Better late than never. With very few exceptions, all the seeds recommended in the foregoing pages can be obtained from them, at very modest prices, from a shilling upwards.

Their catalogue—yours for three shillings, post-free—lies before me as I write. It is the 107th annual edition, it has 128 pages, many of them vividly illustrated in natural colour, and at a rough estimate it lists about 7,000 varieties of seeds. An awe-inspiring volume.

In spite of my remarks about rake-offs, in the introduction, I really feel that Messrs Thompson & Morgan, after so glowing a tribute, should send me a dainty complimentary packet of mustard and cress.

But in all seriousness, this is a great firm, with a great tradition, performing a great service to a great industry.

While we are on the subject of seeds, let us also bring to your attention two specialists in:

UNCOMMON SEEDS

The first is:
> Miss Kathleen Hunter,
> Barcaldine House,
> Connel,
> Argyll,
> Scotland.

I don't know Miss Hunter, but her catalogue—which is a sheer delight—suggests so vivid a picture of her that I am putting her in my next detective novel. I see her in her early forties, on the brusque side, very much a 'lady'—if she will forgive so out-moded an epithet—with keen grey eyes and very sensitive hands. Extremely erudite. (I shall make her the daughter of a professor of botany at Cambridge.) Almost embarrassingly outspoken, and a great champion of lost causes and lame dogs. In the book she will be made to poison a very nasty stockbroker with a rare form of Spanish seaweed. (You are almost certain to find the seeds of this seaweed in her catalogue; she goes in for seaweed fertilizer in a big way.)

Please, Miss Hunter, forgive me, if this portrait in any way maligns you. It is really your fault for writing such enchanting catalogues.

Another recommendation for rare seeds is:
> George B. Roberts,
> Faversham,
> Kent.

Here you can obtain all sorts of *curiosa* from Europe and America which you will not find listed elsewhere. Swiss pansies, for instance, which are about twice the size of ordinary ones.

*   *   *

From seeds, let us turn to:

BULBS

This is the cue for the entrance of:

> The Giant Snowdrop Co.,
> Hyde,
> Chalford,
> Gloucestershire.

If snowdrops mean anything to you, this company must certainly come into your life. They grow nothing but snowdrops, and magnificent specimens they are. I don't think they will ever be very rich because sometimes they have an odd but endearing habit of popping in an extra clump.

If you write to them, write in August. Do not forget the cultural hints in Chapter Three.

DAFFODILS AND OTHER BULBS

There are of course dozens of places where you can buy fine daffodils etc. My own favourites are:

> Walter Blom & Son Ltd,
> Coombelands Nurseries,
> Leavesden,
> Watford,
> Herts.

P. de Jager & Sons (London) Ltd,
Windsor House,
40 Victoria St,
SW1

Wallace & Barr,
The Old Gardens,
Tunbridge Wells,
Kent.

These firms are mentioned in alphabetical order because—
if they will forgive me for saying so—there is not very much to
choose between them in the sense that they are all first-class.

By the way, not every amateur realizes the vast price
commanded by some of the newer daffodils, as I once learnt
at the R.H.S. Daffodil Show. There was a very beautiful
daffodil at £6 a bulb, and I foolishly thought that it was £6
a hundred. I ordered a hundred and was politely handed an
invoice for £600.

Still on the subject of bulbs which, for the sake of argument, we will assume to include corms, let us here bring
within your reach the flower for which I have so great a
personal attachment:

THE WILD GLADIOLUS

The man to write to is:

C. Newberry Esq.,
Bulls Green Nursery,
Knebworth,
Herts.

He deserves a stamped addressed envelope for his very
instructive little four-page pamphlet, which is printed on a
rather sickly shade of pink. When you study it, pause at the
word 'illyricus'. This denotes the true native wild gladiolus,
and you can make it yours for 6s. a dozen.

For the more conventional forms of gladiolus—the great big monsters in all the latest shades, which one has to have because one would be *déclassé* if one hadn't, apply to:

> Kelway & Sons Ltd,
> Langport,
> Somerset.

Maybe I have been unkind to these lanky creatures, because Kelway's have some ravishing examples attired in unexpected shades of blue and lavender and turquoise. Maybe they will come to mean something to me one day, emotionally. At the moment of writing, they don't. They remind me of expensive models, standing with distended nostrils on the staircase of the Savoy Hotel, waiting to be placated with caviar.

LILIES

You can buy two of the American lilies which we have praised so highly from Walter Blom & Son Ltd, whose address has already been given. These are the peerless Green Dragon and the exquisite Pink Perfection. They are not cheap—30s. per bulb at the time of writing. Possibly, by the time these words are printed, they will have come down in price. If you are really smitten by the lily fever you may feel inclined to write to the American king of the lily world:

> Jan de Graaf,
> The Lily Farms,
> Oregon,
> U.S.A.

There are always certain tiresome difficulties about getting bulbs and seeds from abroad, but they are not insuperable.

For the general run of lilies, you cannot do better than de Jager's, or Wallace & Barr, whose addresses have already been given.

This will have to be rather a long section because in it we consider most of the lesser-known plants and trees which have been mentioned in the body of the book.

However there is one tree that has *not* been mentioned—maybe the most important tree in the garden. Why? I hardly know. Whenever I came round to it my attention was diverted elsewhere. And now, here we are in the appendix without having said a word about this glorious thing, which always draws the crowd when the garden is open to the public. Let us hasten to make amends. The name is, *Robinia pseudacacia friesia.*

And the reason for all this excitement is because the leaves are sheer gold. Even on dull days it shines like a light; but when the sun is filtering through the branches the whole tree seems to be flickering with yellow flames.

Now, this is a *new* tree. I doubt whether one British garden in a thousand boasts of a specimen. But if there is one gardening prophecy that can be made with any certainty, it is that this is a tree with a great and glorious future. You can get it—I hope—from Hillier's, who are, of course, one of the leading nurserymen in the world. I believe that there are a few other firms who have a limited supply, but Hillier's is your best bet for it was they who originated it. Their address has already been given.

Here a word of warning should be issued. I was exceptionally lucky in the purchase of my two specimens; by mere chance I happened to be among the first in the field, and was able, on a personal visit, to pick out two beautifully-shaped examples. Some people who came afterwards were not so fortunate; though they got perfectly sound and healthy trees, they were rather of the Maypole variety, so that their purchasers will have to wait a year or two before the side branches develop. However, this is not a really serious drawback for this robinia is one of the fastest growing trees I have ever encountered; we have already had to move several flowering shrubs over which its branches were extending. I don't care. It can take up as much of the garden as it wants. Any gardener who does not make every effort to obtain it should have his head examined.

After the robinia we may mention:

THE EUCALYPTUS TREES

This section is only for the adventurous. After all, it was as the result of an adventure that I obtained my own eucalyptus trees—the twist of the wheel that caused me to drive up the lane of the mysterious nursery where they were growing. I call it 'mysterious' because there is something magic about it; you feel that at any moment you may blink your eyes and find that the whole place has vanished into thin air. All the same, it does actually exist, though it is not at all easy to find. The address is:

> G. Reuthe Ltd,
> Keston,
> Kent.

This is one of the cases where you *must* write and ask them the way, otherwise you will go grinding round a lot of narrow lanes without ever reaching your destination, and end up by having tea on rancid doughnuts in Tunbridge Wells. If Reuthe's have run out of eucalyptus, don't blame me; there will almost certainly be quantities of other rarities which they haven't run out of.

Apart from Reuthe's, I have heard enthusiastic reports of:

> Treseder's Nurseries (Truro) Ltd,
> Truro,
> Cornwall.

C. H. Taudevin Ltd,
Raby Nurseries,
Willaston,
Wirral, Cheshire.

If you feel that the whole thing is a bit too tricky to waste money on, there is always Messrs Thompson & Morgan, the seed merchants, whom we have already mentioned. They supply cheap packets of many varieties, including the fabulous *cordata*. I note that they list this as suitable only for the cool greenhouse. Well, we shall see.

What other things come under the heading of 'rarities'? Flicking back the pages at random, an obvious example is:

THE HARDY ORCHIDS

These are obtainable from two first-rate nurseries:

R. M. Adey,
Frampton Plants,
High Cannons,
Well End,
Barnet,
Herts.

Taplin's,
26 Clarendon Park,
Clacton.

Here we might also mention a man I long to meet because his catalogue is written with such breathless enthusiasm and because it contains so many intriguing oddities—things that you will find nowhere else in Britain.

G. B. Rawinsky,
Primrose Hill Nursery,
Bunch Lane,
Haslemere, Surrey.

Another rarity is the semi-hardy climber with chocolate and tangerine flowers and strange futuristic leaves: *Abutilon milleri.*

This is best obtained from those universal providers, Hillier's of Winchester. This firm will also supply one of my favourite blues: *Pulmonaria angustifolia.*

Another of the blues which we have celebrated is: *Caryopteris 'Ferndown'.*

The finest specimens of this little treasure are supplied by:

> Stewart's Nurseries,
> Ferndown,
> Dorset.

CLEMATIS

Perhaps we are not justified in including the clematis family among the 'rarities', but as I have only mentioned the seldom-grown tangutica at any length, we may be excused for doing so. For this, and indeed for every variety of clematis, your best bet is Messrs Jackman's at Woking, recommended above.

However, there is another clematis firm whose catalogue is well worth getting:

> Fisk's Clematis Nursery,
> Westleton,
> Saxmundham,
> Suffolk.

These are the people who are popularizing the sensationally beautiful lavender variety William Kennett, which is probably the largest clematis in existence. A real traffic-stopper.

For those living in the eastern counties I recommend a personal visit to the admirable firm of:

> Pennell & Sons Ltd, Lincoln.

More rarities? Here, surely, we should mention herbs. Although this book has been mainly concerned with flowers, the reader will probably have guessed that there was a little herb garden in the background. Only a tiny one, for growing the lovage, the mints and sages and thymes, and of course the chives which Gaskin finds so essential. Apart from the remarkable Miss Kathleen Hunter, whose imaginary portrait I drew a few pages back, the most comprehensive collection of herbs is grown by:

> Herb Farm Ltd,
> Seal,
> Sevenoaks,
> Kent.

We are nearing the end of our list of rarities. One of them is most certainly the silver-leaved, *Senecio cineraria maritima*, Ramparts.

You may remember that I described this as the most brilliant example of silver in nature. It is obtainable from:

> Mrs Desmond Underwood,
> Ramparts Nurseries,
> Braiswick,
> Colchester,
> Essex.

Judging from the plants in which she specializes, Mrs Underwood might be described as the Silver Queen. Her displays at the Chelsea Flower Show are always a symphony of silvers and whites and pale greys, with an occasional touch of the palest pink and yellow. A lady of quite exceptional taste.

HEATHERS

Obviously, heathers cannot be numbered among the

exotics. But there *are* unusual and little-grown heathers, and for these you cannot do better than apply to a firm which has been supplying me all my life:

> Maxwell & Beale Ltd,
> Broadstone,
> Dorset.

Many of my friends also speak highly of:

> John F. Letts,
> Heather Specialists,
> Westwood Rd,
> Windlesham,
> Surrey.

Heathers are not cheap; most of the carnea varieties are about 38s. a dozen. However, they are extremely easy to propagate, either by layering or by cuttings. So if you are planning a heather garden I should be inclined to order half a dozen of several varieties, and grow your own families.

THE OLD ROSES

I am not competent to advise about the ordinary run of roses. Who is? There are so many hundreds of nurseries, displaying so many thousands of plants, that your best plan is to visit those that are nearest to you, on a summer afternoon, and choose your own plants.

However, in the case of the old-fashioned roses the range is not nearly so wide. Comparatively few firms grow them in any quantity and you may have to rely on catalogues. In this case I would certainly send three shillings for *The Manual of Shrub Roses* by G. S. Thomas, which is obtainable from:

> Sunningdale Nurseries,
> Windlesham,
> Surrey.

Mr Thomas is one of the leading experts in this field and his *Old Shrub Roses* (Phoenix House Ltd, 32s. 6d.) is recognized as authoritative. The manual is not a catalogue, in the strict sense of the word—the price list is separately printed—but it contains a mine of information and a great deal of descriptive matter so vividly written that the flowers seem to live before you.

Another outstanding catalogue, which might indeed be described as a miniature encyclopaedia, is produced by:

> T. Hilling & Co. Ltd,
> Chobham,
> Surrey.

I can also recommend, particularly for the very old and almost forgotten varieties:

> Edwin Murrell,
> Shrewsbury,
> Shropshire.

RHODODENDRONS

For this section we really need a map of Britain. Our island may be a precious gem, set in the silver sea, but it is a gem with a great many flaws in it, flaws of chalk, a substance for which I have an almost pathological hatred. It is therefore obvious that all the great rhododendron nurserymen must be grouped in areas that are free from this poison; it is equally obvious that I can have only a limited personal experience of these firms. However, for those who live in the south, I can recommend the following: Hillier and Sons. (Address already given.) For extensive range of both species and hybrids. G. Reuthe Ltd. (Address already given.) And:

> Sunningdale Nurseries,
> Windlesham,
> Surrey.

Over 300 species and 600 varieties of rhododendrons and azaleas:

> John Waterer, Sons & Crisp Ltd,
> The Floral Mile,
> Twyford,
> Berks.

Large selection of plants offered at reduced prices during annual spring sales. Renowned for rhododendron hybrids:

> Knap Hill Nursery Ltd,
> Woking,
> Surrey.

Very large stocks including a number of exceptionally large specimens.

At the risk of repeating myself I cannot over-emphasize the importance of choosing your rhododendrons personally, on the spot, even if it means keeping a pair of galoshes permanently in the boot of the car. To buy them only from the catalogue is to ask for trouble; each of these glorious shrubs has a personality of its own—a personality that is expressed in every twist of the branches, every curve of the leaf, every subtlety of the patina that glows on the leaf's underside. To buy a rhododendron, as it were, from cold print is as foolish as to buy an animal from an advertisement. These are living things that either speak to you or don't, and you must be sure that you speak the same language.

AQUATICS

As in the case of the heathers, I have been dealing with the same firm all my life, Messrs Perry's of Enfield. If you are a patron of the Chelsea Flower Show you will almost certainly have been drawn by their delightful pools with the water-plants clustering around them. Their address is:

Perry's Hardy Plant Farm,
Enfield,
Middlesex.

However, I know of two other water gardens created by two other firms, and they are so well-designed and stocked that they deserve a mention:

L. Haig & Co. Ltd,
The Aquatic Nurseries,
Newdigate,
Surrey.

Taylor's Nursery,
Bracknell,
Berks.

Your best course is probably to send for all these catalogues and see which most allures you.

If you are new to the water business you should be warned that although the actual *planting* of such things as water-lilies is simplicity itself, there are one or two tricks of the trade—too technical for these pages—with which you should acquaint yourself before delivery. These tricks are clearly delineated in the catalogues.

Do not forget that aquatics are not sent out till May or early June. This does not mean that your water garden is dead till then; as we have seen, some of the aquatics, like the calthas, will start to flower in March.

And do not forget that they do not like being out of their native element for too long. In other words do not go away for an extra long week-end if there is any danger of the post-man arriving with a rather soggy parcel and being obliged to leave it at the front door.

One last word about catalogues. Please remember that in these days they are increasingly expensive to produce, and that many of them are offered by the nurserymen at a price which is less than the cost of production. If you put in an extra shilling to cover the cost of postage you will be making a nice little gesture to a very ancient and honourable body of men.

AIDS TO GARDENING

When visitors come to see my garden, it is fairly certain that at least fifty per cent of them will inquire how we manage to have such a perfect lawn. I can make this arrogant statement without compunction because, as we have already promised, it is open, on occasions, to inspection. It *is* a perfect lawn. There may be as good lawns on the luxury putting greens of a few millionaires, but there are no better ones. How could there be? On my lawn there is not a weed, not the trace of a bald patch nor a blade of couch grass—nothing but a deep velvety pile of emerald grass which makes you feel that you are walking through the salons of an exceptionally plushy cinema.

How is this done?

It took time. To be precise, all the four years that I have been in residence. At the outset the lawn was a mass of clover, which may be a pretty little thing when it is growing in the wild, but is a rampant pest when it gets into a lawn. We rid ourselves of it by a preparation of which I cannot speak too highly:

Clovotox

This is a May & Baker product, inexpensive and easy to apply. It is, of course, one of the hormones, which act on compounds, on a principle that has always struck me as faintly macabre; they are primarily stimulants and then kill the weeds by making them outgrow their strength. The wretched creatures absorb the stuff greedily, like starving children gobbling poisoned sweets, and for a space they

244

wax, only to wane most pitifully. If there were a Society for the Prevention of Cruelty to Weeds I should almost certainly be one of its vice-presidents; as things are, I use it in large quantities. Which prompts another elemental word of warning—do not use it in *too* large quantities. You may be tempted to do so, if you are of an impatient nature, under the mistaken impression that an extra dosage will hasten the results. It will not. It will only burn an ugly patch which will have to be returfed or resown. Keep strictly to the proportions recommended on the tin.

After the clover we tackled the moss, and here again we had recourse to the excellent Messrs May & Baker, who have perfected the best moss killer I know, called:

Mostox

I repeat, the best moss killer *I* know, personally. There may be others, and there are certainly a host of selective weed-killers worthy of a trial—such as Messrs Fison's admirable Evergreen, which is not only a weedkiller but a dressing. And of course the ever-popular Verdone. I am only going on about Clovotox and Mostox because I am assuming that you are asking me what *we* did, to attain this perfection. And I'm trying to answer that question as simply as possible.

However, no lawn has ever been brought to perfection merely by the aid of science; even if you had at your disposal the entire resources of the I.C.I. you would still need a plentiful supply of that ancient and unpurchaseable commodity—elbow grease. Thus early in every spring we spend at least three days hard work with an instrument that I call a:

Scrabbler

In other words, a lawn rake. Not an inch of the lawn misses the attention of this admirable implement, and the amount of dead grass it drags up is quite astonishing—all the clippings and residue of the previous year, barrowfuls of it, which we throw on to the compost heap. The effect of the scrabbler is so swift as to be almost dramatic; it is as though you could hear the lawn breathing a sigh of relief. But scrabbling is exhausting; it is very much a man's job. It most certainly does not come under the heading of 'A Child Can Do It'—a form of advertisement that always enrages me, particularly when it shows, as it usually does, a grinning and beribboned female infant propelling a steam-roller up a steep hill with her little finger. A muddled illustration, but you probably know what I mean.

We suggested that the lawn 'breathed a sigh of relief'. Well, lawns *do* breathe—like everything else in Nature, from sea anemones to Madame Callas. But sometimes they must be helped to breathe. And here we have to apply yet more elbow grease, with an instrument I call the:

Dibbler

This is really only a fork with hollow prongs, which we prod into the lawn to aerate it. Dibbling is not as exhausting as scrabbling, but it is a first-class bore, and after an hour of it the soul is inclined to revolt. And one begins to ask oneself whether it would not be simpler, in the long run, to have the whole damned thing paved with Yorkshire stone. These interludes of depression can normally be relieved, at least for the time being, by a small injection of:

Gin and Tonic

In gardening, as in most of life's enterprises, there are moments when a moderate consumption of alcohol accelerates one's progress down the garden path.

And this must be the cue for lawn stimulants. We have cleaned the lawn's complexion, and banished the weeds. We have opened the lawn's lungs, and helped it to breathe. But now—continuing the corporeal metaphor—we must fill the lawn's stomach. Few people, when their eyes light on a stretch of green grass, realize that a lawn is a *hungry* thing. All those millions of blades of grass, waiting to be fed! There are wide spaces in the forest, and in even the most closely packed herbaceous border there are merciful gaps, where the sun can reach, and the rain can fall, and generous Mother Earth can accumulate a few reserves of energy for the children that are crowding in upon her with their arid roots. But in a lawn there is no respite; there is not an inch to spare; there is over-population on a scale that outstrips the struggling wastes of China.

And yet, the great majority of gardeners leave their lawns to fend for themselves, to pine and starve and cling to a pitiable life as best they may.

This brings me to the most important of all the things that we put on the lawn:

Velvetone

This was, with both Mr Page and myself, a fairly recent discovery. We had used lawn sand, of course. And fish manure, even though it filled the whole of Ham Common with rancid odours, and brought a wild gleam into the eyes of the cats, who rushed round the garden in a state of continual excitement for three days, as though they were searching for ectoplasmic haddocks. But it was not till Velvetone came into our lives—how, I cannot remember—that the results were really sensational.

A word of advice about this magic product, which comes in two varieties, one for autumn and one for spring and summer. The autumn dressing is rich in phosphates, which stimulate the growth of the roots; the spring and summer dressing is rich in nitrogen, which stimulates top growth. *Both* dressings are therefore vital.

At least, after all this palaver, one thing must surely have emerged—the fact that a perfect lawn does not come of its own volition. Like all things beautiful, and all things civilized, it requires constant vigilance and ceaseless nourishment. If Sir Winston Churchill had ever risen, in a moment of crisis, to defend the green lawns of England—and when one comes to think of it, this is what he actually did—I could have helped him with his peroration. It would have gone, roughly, like this:

'I have nothing to offer you but blood, tears, toil, sweat, Clovotox, Mostox, Scrabbling, Dibbling, Velvetone, Verdone, phosphates, nitrates, May & Baker, Fison's, Imperial Chemicals, old Uncle Tom Cobley and All.'

I have only three other recommendations in this section on aids to gardening, which is extraordinary, considering that the tool-shed is crammed to over-flowing with bottles and gadgets. But one has to draw the line somewhere. The first recommendation, for a general plant tonic and stimulator, is an old favourite.

Sangral

You can really see the results of this liquid manure. It is rather as though you had given a glass of invalid port to a nice old lady and had totted it up with a teaspoonful of navy rum. The plants seem to sit up and take notice.

Last, but one!

Tritox

This really does spell the end of greenfly, and to a whole host of other insect pests, such as caterpillars. You simply water it into the roots, and the poison—which is quite harmless to the plant itself—is absorbed by every twig and leaf so that as soon as the wretched creatures start their nibbling they gasp and fade away. Needless to say you must not use it on vegetables or on any form of plant life destined for human consumption.

Last of all, but by no means least:

Sequestrene

This newcomer has an importance that has yet to be realized by the gardening public. In a moment Mr Page will explain the techniques by which it functions.

Sequestrene might be described as God's gift to those who live on soils that are impregnated with chalk. To the best of my knowledge it is the only product yet invented which can cope with the abominable stuff, and take at any rate the greater part of the sting out of it. For this reason it may greatly widen the horizons of tens of thousands of gardeners, who, until now, have been obliged to deny themselves so many of Nature's treasures. Needless to say, it cannot perform miracles; it will not enable you to grow rhododendrons on the white cliffs of Dover. But it is genuinely effective when the alkaline content is not excessive, as I know from personal experience. The leaves of a number of my own rhododendrons were growing yellow and showing all the evidence of chalk poisoning because their roots had got into the lime which some previous owner had used to make his garden paths. Sequestrene completely stopped the rot in a matter of a few months.

Mr Page is so far more knowledgeable than I am about these matters that I have asked him to explain the principles of this product in his own words. He writes:

Rhododendrons, camellias, ericas and callunas are a few of the many plants which cannot be grown successfully in soils containing a high chalk or lime content. In such soils iron, which is essential in the manufacture of chlorophyll, becomes 'unavailable'. Without this element, plants become chlorotic (i.e. lacking chlorophyll) and the leaves take on a characteristic yellow appearance, particularly between the veins. In extreme cases they may die.

250

APPENDIX

A deficiency of magnesium and manganese may also be a contributory factor.

Sequestrene contains these elements in a form which plants growing in alkaline soils can readily absorb.

The preparation should be applied in early spring, preferably during rainy spells. If applications are made when the soil is dry, thorough watering is essential to ensure that the solution reaches the lower root zone.

The use of Sequestrene should be complementary to the normal gardening practice of planting and mulching with acid organic matter such as peat and leaf soil.

Though it would be an exaggeration to say that Sequestrene is in the experimental stage I understand that it is constantly being improved, and that the manufacturers hope eventually to bring it to an even greater pitch of perfection.

It is obtainable exclusively from:

The Murphy Chemical Co. Ltd,
Wheathampstead,
Herts.

*   *   *

So ends our little book. I am very aware of its inadequacies, but I hope that it may have helped a few gardeners and given them some new ideas. And that it may perhaps encourage some of those who have not yet begun to garden to start out on this great adventure which is, to me, one of the principal reasons for living. As I once wrote, many years ago, in *Down the Garden Path*, a garden is 'the only mistress who never fades, who never fails'.

One last word to those who would like to come and see the flowers I have celebrated, growing in their domestic setting. I made this offer because I have sometimes been not unreasonably piqued by critics who have suggested that my gardening was all theory and no practice. And I have no intention of withdrawing it; the flowers *can* be inspected and 'verified'—within reason. However, I am sure that the kindly reader will realize that the garden is not a public place, even though I have written about it so frankly, and that for most of the days of the year I would like to go on prowling round it in solitude, muttering, and stroking the cats. Apart from that, a garden is a seasonal affair, God wot; I cannot produce lilies in April nor rhododendrons in October, and if any rash person arrived on a summer afternoon, in search of *Iris unquicularis* all I could show him would be a mass of rather rusty green leaves. So perhaps the best idea, for all concerned, would be to write to:

> The Secretary,
> Sudbrook Cottage,
> Ham Common,
> Surrey.

At the risk of sounding faintly like something from Harrods I would suggest that you write GARDEN in the top left-hand corner; and since stamps will probably be ninepence apiece by the time these words are printed it would be only humane to enclose a stamped addressed envelope. If hundreds of people all write at once I cannot imagine what will happen; if nobody writes at all, I shall be deeply pained. Altogether, it seems an explosive situation, but it might—just conceivably might—be fun.

INDEX

The index of plant names was prepared by Roy C. Dicks. Scientific names have been corrected and updated where necessary. Boldfaced numbers indicates pages with illustrations.